Praise for
Centered

"A remarkable story in which family, deep self-reflection, and an unshakable belief in a path predestined by God triumph over fortune and comfort. There truly is no testimony without a test—a point Jason proves many times over in this wonderfully impactful read."

—*John Harbaugh, head coach of the Baltimore Ravens*

"Former NFL player Jason Brown walked away from comfort and familiarity in 2012 to accept a new calling that was out of his comfort zone. As owner of First Fruits Farm in North Carolina, Brown is known today as the Sweet Potato Whisperer. Farming has stretched him and his family yet brought them closer together and benefited countless families in need. The stories Jason shares point to a heavenly Father who loves to bless those who are obedient to His call."

—*James Robison, founder and president of LIFE Outreach International*

"This story chronicles the sacrifices, trials, and ultimately the provision, protection, purpose, and blessings that Jason and Tay Brown found as they left wealth and riches to follow God's call to serve in His kingdom. As Jesus said, 'It is easier for a camel to go through the eye of a needle than for a rich person' to do this. Their lives offer inspiration to everyone, and this book gives pause and a chance for self-reflection of one's own choices and priorities. Jason and Tay Brown are an inspiration of courage, faith, and commitment to God, family, and community."

—*John Mahshie, executive director of Veterans Healing Farm*

"Jason Brown's inspiring journey told in *Centered* is a powerful self-reflection of a life filled with pride, humility, and a series of twists and turns that ultimately drove him and his family to give it all up, only to gain it all back and more, through his dramatic decision to walk by faith and follow God's confusing and, at times, questionable calling. *Centered* is real faith at its core, depicting the challenging pressures of today's society as well as its destructive and thinly veiled version of success. Jason's most honest and vulnerable moments turn today's cultural views upside down and thrust readers into questioning the depth of their own faith and personal relationship with God, forcing them to reexamine their own priorities, beliefs, and choices to live with divine purpose."

—*Chip Paillex, president and founder of America's Grow-a-Row*

"*Centered* is engaging, enlightening, and reflective. Jason tells a very personal story—from being bullied as a child in a racially segregated community to becoming the highest paid center in the NFL, then retiring at the height of his career to follow God's calling for him. His joy and fulfillment from helping others, while overcoming his own despair when his farm was on the verge of bankruptcy, is motivating. This is an excellent read from an inspiring person."

—*Bubba Cunningham, director of athletics at the University of North Carolina*

"Jason Brown's story is bathed in Scripture, and his journey through faith and obedience is cut straight from the Old Testament. Examples of Job, Joseph, and Daniel all come to mind as Jason rises above worldly success and acts obediently to share Christ with the hurting."

—*Edward Graham, Samaritan's Purse*

"Jason Brown's story is a remarkable testament to living a life that exemplifies the true qualities most of us desire but too often fall short of attaining. At age twenty-seven, at the height of his NFL career filled with prestige, fame, and worldly fortune, he walked away from it all. Jason's rock-solid faith led him to farming and a new life, of abundance and blessings for his family and neighbors in need, well beyond anything he could have imagined."

—*Joe Lamp'l, Emmy Award–winning creator and executive producer of* Growing a Greener World *and founder of joegardener.com*

Centered

Centered

TRADING YOUR PLANS
FOR A LIFE THAT MATTERS

JASON BROWN
WITH PAUL ASAY

WATERBROOK

CENTERED

Details in some anecdotes and stories have been changed to protect the identities of the persons involved.

Published in the United States by WaterBrook, an imprint of Random House, a division of Penguin Random House LLC.

WATERBROOK® and its deer colophon are registered trademarks of Penguin Random House LLC.

Author is represented by Alive Literary Agency, www.aliveliterary.com.

All photographs, with the exception of those credited, are courtesy of the author's personal archives.

Library of Congress Cataloging-in-Publication Data
Names: Brown, Jason, 1983- author. | Asay, Paul, author.
Title: Centered : trading your plans for a life that matters / Jason Brown with Paul Asay.
Description: First edition. | Colorado Springs : WaterBrook, 2021.
Identifiers: LCCN 2020022396 | ISBN 9780593193358 (hardcover) | ISBN 9780593193365 (ebook)
Subjects: LCSH: Obedience—Religious aspects—Christianity. | Vocation—Christianity. | Brown, Jason, 1983- | Farmers—Religious life—North Carolina. | Christian biography. | African American football players—Biography.
Classification: LCC BV4647.O2 B755 2021 | DDC 270.092 [B]—dc23
LC record available at https://lccn.loc.gov/2020022396

Printed in the United States of America on acid-free paper

waterbrookmultnomah.com

9 8 7 6 5 4 3 2 1

First Edition

Interior book design by Diane Hobbing

SPECIAL SALES Most WaterBrook books are available at special quantity discounts when purchased in bulk by corporations, organizations, and special-interest groups. Custom imprinting or excerpting can also be done to fit special needs. For information, please email specialmarketscms@penguinrandomhouse.com.

Tay,
My crown and worthy of all my love.
Oh, what a blessing you are!
Such a fruitful vine, and our children are your vigorous fruits.
Our family flourishes because of your faithfulness.
More than a helpmate, you are my armor bearer who
oftentimes fearlessly charges into battle.
If only the world could see that you are the real hero
and I'm only a sidekick!

Contents

Centered

CHAPTER 1

Stuck

Be careful what you pray for. The thought crept into my mind as I squinted through the cloud of mayflies and mosquitoes buzzing all around me, biting me, sucking me dry.

I was in the middle of my farm in 2014, mowing fields on an ancient tractor that wheezed and growled as I ran over and cut and crushed the stubborn Carolina growth. *Brush hogging,* they call it, and the job's just as tough and ugly as it sounds. The sun beat down on me like a mallet. Sweat ran down my face, turning my shirt as wet as a washcloth. Dust billowed up from the parched ground in angry, empty clouds, the grit coating my clothes, my hat, my skin.

It got inside me too. With each breath, I sucked in Carolina dirt. Every time I blew my nose, black mess came out.

I prayed for this, I thought. I gave up mansions and millions for this. I gave up comfort and luxury and a career that countless kids all over America dream of. *For this.* A kingdom of mosquitoes and dust. And the land, like the mosquitoes, was slowly sucking me dry.

. . .

Two years earlier, that land looked like heaven to me. To own and run a farm was more than a dream; it was my calling. And I believed in that calling so much that I was willing to throw away a lucrative career in the National Football League to follow it. This was what God wanted me to do: for my wife, Tay, and me to give up our comfortable lives and sink our hands deep into family and faith and the good earth. We followed God's call here, away from a mansion in St. Louis to a broken-down farmhouse in North Carolina and a thousand acres of trees and fishponds and rich, rolling farmland. In October 2012, we bought this little corner of Carolina. And when I stepped onto the property for the first time as its owner with Tay and my oldest son, five-year-old JW, I couldn't contain myself.

"God has blessed us with a place flowing with milk and honey!" I shouted.

JW looked around and frowned. "I don't see any milk," he said, "and I don't see any honey."

I bent beside him, wrapped one arm around him, and pointed with the other to the land we now owned.

"Hey, son," I said. "See those pastures full of green grass?"
He nodded.

"Those pastures can supply food for cows that make the milk we drink. And see all those beautiful wildflowers?"

"Yes, Dad."

"Bees love those wildflowers," I said. "They buzz over to each flower and gather pollen, which they take back to their hives to make honey."

JW smiled. "I get it now, Dad."

He looked over the farm with a bit of wonder on his face. His new home was a living illustration of God's design and provision. On this plot of land, God's greatness and His goodness were on display for *everyone* to see, even a five-year-old on the verge of a strange new chapter in his life. I could see it too. I could *feel* it.

Jesus said in Matthew 6:33, "Seek first the kingdom of God and his righteousness, and all these things will be added to you." Tay and I prayerfully sought out the kingdom, and the righteousness, of God. And this—this corner of Eden—is what was added to us. A blessing. A gift.

But sometimes even God's most precious, most miraculous gifts come with little asterisks attached. Sunshine is a gift, but too much sun and your crops will wither. Rain is a gift, but too much rain and the crops will be stunted or wash away. Children are gifts as well, but no parent on God's green earth will tell you they're easy to give birth to or easy to raise.

In 2012, Tay and I had our land flowing with milk and honey.

Two years later, we knew it was filled with sweat and tears too.

By that summer, the summer of 2014, Tay and I were pretty much broke. Everything we'd counted on to get First Fruits Farm up and running was gone—evaporated like a puddle of water on a hot, dry summer day. Milk and honey? All I could see was the dust. I couldn't wait for our financial situation to get better. We needed to plant. And though a farm our size needs a really good tractor, I didn't have enough money for even a bad one. So I borrowed a hand-me-down dinosaur of a tractor, a 1968 Allis-Chalmers, from my father.

It should've been in a museum. Maybe it's a miracle the thing ran at all. It was fifteen years older than I was, and it had rolled off the assembly line years before the Beatles broke up.

Heck, the Allis-Chalmers company itself went out of business before I graduated from high school. Sentimental farmers might keep an old warhorse like that running, but typically, fifty-year-old tractors don't do much more than gather cobwebs and sprout rust.

Sometimes when another farmer came to visit or I ran into one in town, I'd try to glean all the wisdom I could from him, and during the conversation, I'd always mention my borrowed tractor.

"I'm hoping I'll be able to make it work for a while," I'd say. "Can I be a successful farmer with a tractor like this?"

Some would shake their heads. Some would laugh. More than one of them said, "Jason, if I had that big farm of yours, I'd go out of business with that tractor."

I'd go out of business with that tractor.

I thought about it as I rode that tractor that hot, dusty day. Acres and acres of brush and dark, dry dirt spread in every direction. Another mosquito bit the back of my neck. The sun felt as strong as a jackhammer. And I knew right then that going out of business was a real possibility. *Possibility?* Some might've looked at our situation and said it was all but guaranteed.

The tractor wasn't going to last forever. It might not last the afternoon. I thought about the money I'd sunk into the farm already. I thought about the money I'd set aside that was supposed to equip and staff the farm—the cash that, through an almost unbelievable string of setbacks, had vanished. I thought about what I could've had if I'd stayed in the NFL: houses and cars and financial security for my kids and my wife and me. I thought about my family and how much they'd already sacrificed to share my dream.

Everyone thought I was crazy when I turned my back on the

NFL to follow God and become a farmer. Was I about to show them that they were right?

The field was empty except for me and my tractor and this sea of dust—the dust I'd sacrificed so much for.

No one was within a mile of me. I was all alone.

But not really.

"God!"

I shouted it above the tractor's wheezes and gasps.

"God! I cried again, turning my face up to the sun and empty sky. "I don't mind praying to You, but every time I get on this thing, do I have to pray that it starts up?"

No voice from above. The cicadas buzzed, the mosquitoes whined, but I didn't hear a thing from God.

This is my life now, I thought. *This is what I gave up my career and my wealth and my glory for. No playoff runs. No cheering fans. Just me and dirt and mosquitoes. If I'm lucky. If I don't lose it all.* I could feel the tears in my eyes.

I was tired and scared and furious with God. I was close to despair. I cried out in my pain, anger, and desperation. I felt as though He had forsaken me.

I didn't hear Him, but I knew He was there. I still believed He had an amazing journey ahead of me, just as He'd made the journey behind me. From a big fat kid to an NFL starter to a clueless farmer, God was plotting my path one strange step at a time. And I was just as amazed as anyone about where it would lead.

CHAPTER 2

Planting

The earth—the ground and dirt and dust we walk on—is part of us. The Bible says so. Right in Genesis 2, we're told that God "formed the man of dust from the ground and breathed into his nostrils the breath of life" (verse 7). And ever since Eden, we've needed to work that dust and dirt to survive. Our very lives depend on it. "By the sweat of your face you shall eat bread, till you return to the ground, for out of it you were taken; for you are dust, and to dust you shall return" (3:19).

Farming, pulling life from the ground, isn't easy. My family farmed for generations. They all felt the sweat on their faces as they plowed and planted and harvested. Farming is a part of my history as far back as we can trace.

But being a black farmer, especially before and during the civil rights movement, came with not just the promise of sweat but also the fear of blood.

My grandfather Jasper Brown owned a two-hundred-acre farm near Yanceyville, North Carolina—a farm just about eighty minutes from where I live now. He grew up farming. He raised four children on that farm. He knew how hard farming was, being at the mercy of the weather and your equipment and the volatile markets. If Jasper's farming experience is anything like mine, he never knew what any year might hold for him. If everything cooperated, he might grow a bumper crop. But if something went wrong, he probably wondered how he'd keep his family—his wife and four growing kids—fed.

I don't know whether or not my grandfather loved being a farmer. But I do know that he wanted to give his own children a choice he never had: the choice to *leave* the farm if they wanted to, to make their own way in classrooms or boardrooms or air-conditioned offices.

But that meant that they'd need an education—a good one. And in the late 1950s and early '60s, the schools in Caswell County were still segregated, as was the case in much of the South. My grandfather wanted to change that.

Yanceyville wasn't unusual. All across the South, the civil rights movement was budding and growing. African Americans were pushing for their God-given rights that had been withheld for so long. But change is never easy, and that sort of change frightened and angered many white southerners. And some, including the powerful Ku Klux Klan, were determined to stop progress by any means possible. As Yanceyville started moving toward school desegregation, the KKK threatened local black leaders and civil rights activists. They even printed notices in the local newspaper. The message was, "If you put your black children in our schools, we're going to hang you."

These weren't idle threats. Black men were regularly harassed and beaten, and lynchings were still happening all across the South. Churches were being burned to the ground. And very often, local law enforcement would just look the other way. So, when a push toward desegregation started gath-

ering steam and the KKK began posting threats in the local
paper, everyone took them very seriously. Black leaders were
scared, and many—including the president of the local chapter of the National Association for the Advancement of Col-
ored People—resigned, fearing for themselves and their
families.

But my grandfather was a farmer. He'd stared down
droughts and floods, and he wasn't about to be frightened off
by men in sheets. After the local president stepped down, Jasper volunteered to lead the NAACP—and the charge for desegregation.

From that moment on, his farm was under siege.

My dad, Lunsford Bernard Brown, was just about twelve at
the time. He and his older brother, Nathan, started working in
the fields armed—carrying a shotgun and a .22 rifle, just in
case of trouble. One day, Dad woke up and saw that someone
had hung a noose in a tree right outside their farm. Everyone
knew that noose was for Jasper Brown.

Late one night, my dad and Nathan were cleaning their guns
when they saw sparks in the woods around the farm, flickering
like a massive candle, sending shadows billowing around the
trees like ghosts. They didn't think much about it at first, my
father tells me, but the light kept getting closer. So they pointed
their guns right at the sparks and fired.

"Drop it, man!" they heard someone shout from the trees.
"Drop it! Run!"

Boom!

Nathan and Lunsford were almost knocked backward from
the sound of the explosion. The sparks were coming from a lit
stick of dynamite. To this day, even after nearly sixty years,
there's a crater on my grandfather's old property where the
dynamite landed.

The dynamiters were never caught, but we knew they'd

planned to blow up my grandfather's house and everyone in it: my grandpa, grandma, father, uncle, and aunts. If those dynamiters had succeeded, I wouldn't be here.

But none of that deterred my grandfather. He kept pushing, kept crusading, kept applying for transfers to send his children to Bartlett Yancey, the all-white school located just two blocks from the all-black Caswell County Training School. Finally, on January 22, 1963, Jasper dropped his children—including my father—off at Bartlett Yancey. It should've been a day for celebration. Instead, my grandfather feared for his life. And he had reason to.

The rest of that day is a pretty involved story—one that my mom, Deborah, actually wrote about in her own book, *Dead-End Road*. But in short, here's what happened.

Everyone figured my grandfather might be a target that day, but he couldn't just barricade himself at the farm. Shortly after he dropped his children off at school, he drove to the dry cleaner to pick up his shirts. The gentleman behind the counter gave Jasper a bag holding Jasper's fresh laundry.

"Hold it from the bottom," the gentleman told him. "The clothes are heavy."

Well, Jasper didn't think much of that curious comment—at least that's how my family tells it. He just took the bag of laundry out to his car and started heading back to his farm.

Out of nowhere—as Jasper was driving the normally empty narrow road back to the farm—two cars appeared, chasing him and eventually pulling even with him and forcing his car off the road. Several young white men piled out of the cars. Many of them were holding baseball bats and clubs. All of them were shouting obscenities.

"Nigger, we're gonna kill you!" they said, getting out of their cars and running toward my grandfather's. One of the men swung his baseball bat, like he was going for a home run, and smashed the driver's-side window, sending sharp shards of glass flying—over the seat, over the dashboard, over my grandfather.

"We're gonna kill you, nigger," the man with the bat repeated as he reached through the broken glass to unlock the door, and he meant it. Those men were going to beat my grandfather half to death before hanging him. Jasper couldn't run, as his car was surrounded by now. He couldn't beg for mercy—not from these shouting, screaming men. He wanted to give his children a better education, and with it, opportunities that he'd never had. Now it looked as though that gift might cost Jasper everything.

But Jasper was a God-fearing man, a great man of faith. He was a praying man. And so, in that moment, as one of the white men opened the car door, he did the only thing he could: he grabbed the steering wheel so hard that his knuckles turned white, put his head down, and started praying.

The white man reached in. Jasper's eyes were shut, his hands clenched around the wheel, his mind grasping for the God of salvation.

And then God answered Jasper in his prayer.

Hold it from the bottom, he remembered the dry cleaner telling him. *The clothes are heavy.*

Jasper reached over to the bag of clothes and found, in the bottom of the bag, a fully loaded .38 revolver.

He pulled out the gun just before one of the men grabbed his shoulder to drag him out of the car. He pointed the .38 and pulled the trigger, the crack of the shot snapping across the North Carolina sky. A bullet tore through the shoulder of one man, pushing him back.

My grandfather pulled the trigger again. *Bam!* This time the slug grazed someone's temple. The rest of them were more than scared; they were astounded. Before the attack, before my grandfather went to the cleaner's, he'd been stopped by the local police and frisked—just to make sure, I think, he didn't have any weapons. My grandfather's attackers were shocked he had a gun. "This nigger's got a gun in there!" one said. "How'd he get it?"

The assailants ran away, and—thanks to a neighbor and some pretty clever subterfuge—my grandfather successfully went into hiding that day and night, until he could manage safe passage home. He couldn't go to the police, because he feared that they would've just turned him over to the KKK. And he was probably right: his attackers never stood trial, but Jasper did. He was given a ninety-day prison sentence for possession of a deadly weapon. He was ordered to pay court costs, too, plus $244 to pay the medical bills for the people he'd shot. The court deferred the sentence long enough for him to have enough time to harvest his crops.

But the courts, as far as some folks in Caswell County were concerned, didn't settle anything. In their eyes, my grandfather was guilty—guilty of being black and insisting on desegregation, if nothing else. White buyers wouldn't do business with him anymore. The family wasn't safe. The KKK was still out for blood, and it seemed it was just a matter of time before the Browns were attacked again. And this time, no hidden .38 would save them.

On November 22, 1963, President John F. Kennedy was assassinated. While everyone in the county was mourning and distracted, the Browns—my grandmother and her four children, since Jasper was still serving out his sentence—loaded up everything in their farm truck and got out of town. They didn't turn back and went all the way to Washington, DC. Efforts to fully desegregate the area's schools left with them: Caswell County's schools were among the last in the country to complete the process, something that didn't happen until 1969.

It was over. After generations of Browns had lived and farmed in North Carolina, our roots had been yanked out of the earth. They'd been chased away—maybe gone, they thought, for good.

But North Carolina, for all its difficult history, was home to us. Its earth gets in your veins. And God had other plans.

Daddy Issues

The District of Columbia was home for the Browns for a while after that. My dad spent his teen years there and met my mom there, too, even though she'd also grown up on a North Carolina farm. They were married in DC. My sister and older brother were born there. My dad worked for the city government there, eventually becoming Washington's chief landscaping architect. Looking back, it must've been a pretty good job.

But making a living is different from making a life. And for all its monuments and museums and beautiful buildings, DC was a hard place to live back in the early 1980s, when I was about to come along. Gangs were fighting over blocks of land. Crack cocaine had become an epidemic. The whole city was turning really, really bad. And my mother didn't want her children in that sort of environment. She didn't think DC was anyplace to raise a family. So she took us kids and moved to be near her own family back in North Carolina. She moved down to a little town called Henderson, just about forty minutes northeast of Durham and close to the Virginia border.

I was born there on May 5, 1983, back in the state my family had called home for so long. I grew up and graduated in Henderson, and I had a pretty decent childhood.

But I was missing one important thing in my life: my daddy. When the rest of the family moved down to Henderson, my father stayed behind in Washington. There weren't many great jobs in Henderson, not ones that paid as well as the one my father had, at any rate. While we lived in North Carolina, he worked up north, and not just for the government. He was a freelance landscaper too. My dad would work farmer's hours, from dawn to dark, planting and pruning and cutting grass. And everything he made—practically every penny—he'd send back home.

My father has always had an amazing work ethic, and he's always fought for our family, trying to do what's best for us, just like *his* daddy did. Working in Washington (and living away from us) was what my father thought he had to do.

But while that might've been fine for the bottom line, most families don't work well that way. The Browns' bank account was doing just fine, but the Browns were not.

My mom might've had it the worst of all of us. It's hard enough to raise a family when there are *two* parents in the home. As every single parent knows, it's so much harder, exponentially harder, to handle everything with one. With my father essentially out of the picture, my mother had to pick up the slack. She almost needed a split personality: one minute, she had to put on her maternal face, loving and comforting her three children and encouraging us as best she could; and then, another minute, when we needed correction, she had to step into the role of a father figure. It definitely wasn't easy for her.

But it wasn't easy on us kids, either. And as someone who was pretty much raised, practically speaking, in that single-parent household and whose dad was working more than two hundred miles away, I felt unsettled much of the time.

My father would spend two weekends a month at the house in Henderson, and when I was younger, that's all the time I got with him: four days out of every thirty. I never knew a time as a child when my father was really around. And when he *was* around, I didn't know how to respond to him. It was different for my brother, Ducie, and my sister, Dana. They were older than I was. They remembered when our father was a consistent presence in the house. So, when he'd come back to Henderson and walk through our front door, they'd run to him. "Daddy! Daddy!" they'd squeal. But to me, in those early formative years of mine, "Daddy" was more or less a stranger to me. I didn't know how to act around him. I didn't know how to be.

My parents weren't divorced. They weren't even legally separated. They lived apart, but they were still very much married. And as I grew a little older and watched my friends playing with their own fathers, it was a hard thing to explain to people, especially kids my own age.

"Jason, where's your daddy?" people would ask me.

"He's in Washington, DC," I'd always say.

"Oh, so your parents are divorced?"

"No, they're not divorced," I'd snap.

"Yeah, but he ain't never around. He don't even live nowhere near here."

They were right. And even though I knew why he wasn't around, those questions still hurt. Every single time someone asked, it was like a knife to the gut. *Jason, where's your daddy?*

I started asking that same question. Where *is* my daddy? I didn't know why he had to spend so much time away from us. Even going into my teenage years, I didn't completely understand the separation. It seemed like every time he'd come to North Carolina, I'd ask him when he was staying for good.

"Daddy, when are you coming home?" I'd ask. "When are you going to be able to retire?"

He said that the government wouldn't let him retire just yet. I didn't understand what it meant to have a pension or a retirement account. I didn't know what adults needed to do to make a living and provide for their families. All I knew was that I wanted a daddy.

My father was working hard for us, and I realized that. But it didn't help, any more than knowing how you broke a bone makes it feel better. My dad might've been working hard *there,* but I needed him *here.* It would've been nice to have him around to help with my homework or take me fishing or play catch with me. I didn't care that my father was putting food on the table. I wanted my *daddy* at that table—even with less food, even in a smaller house, even without some of the good things that he'd provided for us. I didn't care if we had a table at all.

I think I carried that hurt for a long time.

I was sixteen when my dad finally retired and came back home to Henderson. My brother and sister were out of the house, so it was just my mom and me. I'm sure Mom was thrilled to have him back, but for me it was strange to have him around after he'd been gone from my day-to-day life for so long. I'd taken on a lot of responsibilities in his absence. I'd grown up, in many ways, without him. So when my dad came back, I felt like he was out of place. *I'm the man of the house,* I thought. *Who are you?*

But even when my dad was away, he was teaching me something: that being a father is more than being just a provider. And on those nights when I was sad and lonely and angry with my father for not being there, I promised myself something: I swore that I would *never* do that to my family. Never.

I don't care what kind of job it is, I told myself. *I don't care what kind of benefits it has. I will never put a job in front of my family. I will always be there for them, no matter when or where. I will always be there.*

But that wasn't the only thing my dad was teaching me.

Green Thumb

My brother and I spent many of our summers in Washington, DC, helping our dad. I saw his work ethic for myself—how he'd wake up for work every day by six. While Ducie and I just stayed at the house all morning, eating cereal and watching cartoons, he'd be out working on the city's trees and lawns and flower beds for his day job. Then, as the clock rolled closer to midafternoon, we'd start listening for his truck and get ready for our *own* workday. We knew that as soon as he pulled up, our dad would be ready to hook up the trailer and start job number two—his freelance landscaping business—and Ducie and I were his best (and only) employees.

Man, did my dad get his money's worth. We worked hard those afternoons, sweating like crazy in those sweltering DC summers. We mowed lawns. We designed flower beds and planted shrubs and trees. Over those summers, I learned how to make things beautiful. I learned how to landscape and garden on a small scale. I didn't know at the time that God was doing His own gardening in me—planting a seed or two that would only start to really grow ten or fifteen years later. All I knew then was that working the land was hard work, but rewarding work. As much as I might've preferred staying inside and watching cartoons all day, I enjoyed the smell of freshly cut grass, the feel of the dirt in my hands, and the pride that comes with taking a plot of raggedy land and, through hard work and planning, making it into something better.

And although my father might not have been with us much in North Carolina, a piece of him was. We could look out the window and see it.

When my mom decided that she wanted to go back to North Carolina to raise their family, she and my dad decided to do it right. Since they were both farm kids at heart, home just didn't feel like home without a *little* land attached. They invested in about a forty-acre spread—not really a farm, but just a little homestead that they could work and enjoy. And my dad, when they first bought the place and on his visits home, would putter around back there, improving it a little at a time.

He planted trees in our backyard: pear trees and nut trees and, especially, apple trees. Every year, I watched them come into bloom and blossom, covering the branches with their fragrant flowers. The flowers didn't last long, but another sort of beauty would follow right on their heels: they'd start growing fruits. Most children today don't get a chance to see something like that—to truly watch trees shed their flowery springtime beauty and grow those tasty little miracles. But I did. I would see those tiny apples grow and grow, each day looking a little bigger, a little sweeter. I saw the miracle of food right in our backyard.

Maybe those two elements were the beginning of my future career: learning how rewarding working with the land can be and seeing the fruits of your labor grow right before your eyes.

Sometimes as I was growing up, I'd ask my mom for some money or to buy me a toy or something, like every kid does. And, like every mother does, my mom would say, "Do you think money grows on trees?"

"No," I admitted one day, "but *food* does."

She glared at me and told me to stop being smart. But you know what? It was true. Food *does* grow on trees. And food has value—not just value in keeping us alive and healthy, but monetary value. The green apples, I knew already, were something of value that grow on trees. Something you can not only see and smell and feel but also taste. And cook. And sell.

Even back then, when farming was about the last thing I ever thought I'd be doing with my life, I understood the miracle behind it. I understood how beautifully God designed the world—how He gave us everything we'd need in the soil and seeds if we just learned how to grow it and get it.

Again, "by the sweat of your face you shall eat bread, till you return to the ground, for out of it you were taken; for you are dust, and to dust you shall return" (Genesis 3:19), God told Adam and Eve that terrible day in Eden when the two walked out of the garden for good. We call it the Fall—the day when God and men were separated by sin, Eden was closed to us, and the seeds for suffering and misery and disaster were sown in the world.

But in that moment, when God showed His hard justice to Adam and Eve and the rest of us, He showed His mercy too. He might've locked away paradise, but He also gave us the keys for something else: the ability to farm and live.

The life of a farmer isn't easy, and it's *far* from paradise. I feel the sweat on my face nearly every day. I feel my muscles ache and the bone-hard weariness in every fiber of my body.

But when I grow something, I see a reminder of that holy garden sometimes—the echo of what could've been. As a boy, I felt that echo for the first time.

Life wasn't easy; I knew that already, even as a kid. My father was gone so much. I knew how hard he had to work to keep a roof over his family's head and food on the table.

But I also saw that *food grows on trees*. I knew, even if I wasn't able to fully articulate it then, that the food was a gift from God. Not only was my earthly father working hard for us, but our heavenly Father was providing too. No, our lives were no Eden. That garden was gone. But when I watched those apples grow a little bigger each day, I saw God's provision and plan. Those apples grew, just like we're supposed to do—in body, and in mind, faith, and trust in Him.

I didn't suspect, as a child, that ultimately my future would be so closely tied to growing food that I'd become a farmer, growing crops not that far away from where my grandfather Jasper did. I didn't know I'd be looking to the dust and the dirt to feed not only my family but countless others as well.

First I had another sort of field to explore.

CHAPTER 3

Brothers

Most people who become pro-caliber football players loved the sport from the time they were babies. They grew up throwing the football with their dads. They played on Pee Wee teams. They were jocks from the time they could tie their shoes—the cool kids on the elementary playground and in the middle school cafeteria.

That wasn't me. I was the fat kid getting bullied by a girl a third my size.

Her name was Britney, and I lived in terror of her. It was fall 1996, and we were both at Eaton-Johnson Middle School. I was just thirteen. That summer, an Eddie Murphy movie called *The Nutty Professor* came out. Murphy played a guy named Sherman Klump, a kindly science professor who'd break the weight scales if he ever stood on one. Britney must've loved that movie. Or, at the very least, she sure loved telling me how much I looked like Sherman Klump.

"Sherman!" she'd holler down the halls. "Sherman, Sherman, Sherman! Why are you so fat, Jason Brown?"

People often think of bullies as the big kids who could just roll up their sleeves and punch the lights out of anyone—and look for any excuse to do so. This skinny little girl couldn't punch the lights out of a lamp. I could've picked her up and snapped her in two like a toothpick. But it didn't matter. "Sherman!" she'd holler, and my blood would run cold. "Sherman!" she'd scream, and I'd start to blush. Every day she bullied me. Every day she called me names. If I saw her before she saw me, I'd start walking fast the other way. It got to the point that if I was walking from building to building, I'd stop and look around the corner to make sure she wasn't there, as if she were a rabid dog. I was walking in constant fear.

If I'd been into sports at the time, maybe she would've left me alone. Jocks seem to get passes in school. But I wasn't a jock. I was about as far away from being a jock as you could be. In fact, I was kind of a loser. I lost at everything I did, it seemed. Especially to my big brother.

Ducie

My brother was named Lunsford Bernard Brown II, after my father. But instead of calling him Junior, everyone just called him Ducie because he was number two. He was our family's free spirit—an artist in talent and temperament. He could draw the most beautiful things in the world, be it a fantastic and elaborate comic-book land or the backyard right outside our house. His hands were always busy with something. If he wasn't drawing something, he was making something, and as we got older, those hands sometimes put aside pencil and paper and picked up hammer and nails. Ducie knew all about carpentry and stonework and masonry—skills that came in handy when he and I helped our dad with his landscaping business. My brother was a natural creator, a builder. And, in many ways, he helped build me too.

Ducie was seven years older than I was, and I idolized him. But here's the deal: *he was seven years older,* and every younger sibling knows that means that when we were both home looking for something to do, Ducie called the shots.

He loved to watch *Star Trek,* so every afternoon that's what we'd watch. I didn't think that sci-fi stuff made much sense, and I got pretty tired of seeing Klingons every time we turned on the TV, but I still watched. He loved video games too. He started out with a Super Nintendo and the SEGA Genesis. But when the family got a PlayStation, he found his real passion. He'd play those games for hours—until four or five in the morning sometimes. As soon as his grades would slip, my mother would take the games away, and then his grades would improve. He'd get his games back, and the grades would slip again. And so it went.

He became a master at those video games, and a kid like me just couldn't keep up. He'd tell me to play a fighting game with him—something like *Street Fighter* or *Mortal Kombat*—and he'd just beat me with ease every single time. He knew all the moves. He was so much quicker than I was. Other kids might've thought, *Well, I just have to practice and get better,* but there was no way I was going to practice more than Ducie. It was hopeless. And because he beat me so badly every time we played, it took all the fun out of it for me.

Video games weren't the only things I lost at. In fact, when I was a kid, it felt like I was the Browns' biggest loser. Even when I sat down and played cards with other family members— even straight-up games of chance, like War—I seemed to lose every single time. *I've got bad luck,* I'd tell myself. But luck or no, it didn't do my ego any good—or help me develop a love for games of chance of any kind. As an adult, I've been to Las Vegas a couple of times, and I've walked through my share of casinos, but my memory of losing as a child is so strong that none of it holds any temptation for me. Zero. I don't trust my luck.

Maybe that's why I didn't turn to sports right away. That, or the fact that my family just wasn't interested in them. My grandfather Jasper wanted to give his own children a better education than he had, and my dad had taken that lesson to heart. My parents knew that school—not sports—was the key to success. If athletics entered their minds at all, it was purely an afterthought.

And even when I *did* try sports, I didn't have much luck in that, either.

My favorite sport is, hands down, *baseball,* not football. I loved to play baseball—and still do, in fact. I'd even played a year of Little League. So, when I went into middle school, I tried out for the baseball team. I did everything I could to make the Eaton-Johnson Middle School team.

I failed. I was cut before the season even began. Man, I was crushed. I'd tried so hard. I'd put so much effort into making that team. It might've been one of the biggest letdowns of my life.

All that losing takes a toll on you. By the time Britney was screaming, "Sherman!" at me in middle school, I was at an all-time low in terms of self-confidence. I felt like the least popular kid at school—a total loser in everything.

You'd think that when Ducie and my sister, Dana, left for college, things would get better. At least I wouldn't be getting thumped playing War and *Mortal Kombat* all the time. But I did feel pretty lonely.

My dad was in Washington, DC. My mom was a real estate agent in the Henderson area and very active politically. She served for sixteen years on the school board and then served another twelve as a county commissioner—the first woman to hold that title, and the first African American too. Those duties kept her away for quite a bit of the time, so I'd come home, make myself a couple of peanut-butter-and-jelly sandwiches, and watch some MTV or maybe a few *Brady Bunch* reruns. Alone.

But that time alone wasn't wasted. I didn't wallow in self-pity—at least not much. Once *The Brady Bunch* was through for the day, I had time to start thinking about what I was going to do with my life. Maybe it was boredom. Maybe it was the fact that I always saw my parents working so hard to better themselves and our family. Maybe there was just something in me that pushed me to think about my future more than most kids my age did. Whatever it was, at the age of thirteen, I started thinking about what my priorities should be.

Faith, I figured, would always be number one in my life. My family had always valued faith so much, and I knew what the Bible said: "Seek ye first the kingdom of God, and his righteousness; and all these things shall be added unto you" (Matthew 6:33, KJV). That was obviously the best place to start.

Family came next. I love my family. I knew I'd lay my life down for any of them. I knew, from my father's absence, how important being with family was to me, so that was definitely number two.

Third was *education*. With my upbringing, how could it not be?

So that was it: faith, family, and education. I committed those goals to memory before I was even shaving.

But by the time I was heading into high school, I was also tired of being picked on by the Britneys of the world. I was tired of losing all the time. I was tired of being the chunky low man on the social totem pole. So I decided to do something pretty ambitious: I was going to be part of the high school band and try out for the football team too.

Tooting My Own Horn

Looking back, it was pretty dumb to do both. We had two-a-day football practices, each one around two hours long. Band practice was nearly *three* hours. I'd be at school the entire day and into the evening. And after three or four days of that, I knew something had to give. Something was bound to break inside me if I kept going down that path. I had to quit one or the other, and the answer seemed simple.

Football had to go.

Football practice was *hard,* man. It was really physically demanding, and I wasn't in great shape to begin with. It was mentally demanding too. My coach, Randy Long, saw that I had potential underneath all my extra fat. He told me that I might make the varsity squad as a freshman. As soon as some of the juniors and seniors heard that, they started hazing me.

At most football practices, you'll see bags or dummies that serve a variety of purposes. When they're laid flat on the ground, you hop and hurdle over them and they become great tools to improve footwork. Stand them on end and have a football player brace them from behind, and they serve as tackling dummies. Well, being the big kid that I was, I was often holding and bracing those dummies for some of the other players. Whenever that happened, the older kids would charge at it—and me—like I'd insulted their mothers. They'd try to knock me flat on my back. I got tired of being a punching bag.

Playing in the marching band was a *lot* easier. I had experience in it, for one thing: I'd played trombone for my middle school band, and I liked it. And while band practice was long and tiring in its own way, at least I wasn't going to get many bruises from it. Plus, marching band had (naturally) many more girls. I thought that maybe I'd be able to hang out with some of them.

At the end of that first grueling week, I walked up to Coach Long and did something I hardly ever do: I quit. I explained to him that I wasn't ready to be a football player. Not yet.

"I'm out of shape, okay?" I told him that morning. "I've got so much baby fat and stuff on me." I'd spend my freshman year getting rid of that baby fat, I told him. I'd work out and work hard to turn that blubber into muscle. Then, once I was ready, I'd try out for the football team again next year.

Coach Long didn't believe me. He looked at me, and I could tell that the only word he really heard from me was *quit*. If there's a sin in sports, that's the biggest. "Once a quitter, always a quitter" goes the cliché, and in that moment, Coach Long pegged me as a quitter. He took my shoulder pads and probably never expected me to walk into his office, for any reason, again.

Unfortunately, marching band wasn't all I hoped it would be either. Sure, there were a lot more girls in band, but I soon discovered they were all looking at the football players. Just being a part of the band stuck me automatically in the friend zone. I gave up on dating anyone there—dating anyone, really—for a while.

Even if Coach Long thought I quit on the team, I hadn't quit on football.

I knew I had to get in shape, become stronger, and lose my baby fat. Lifting weights would be the best way to do it, but I couldn't take a weight-training course my freshman year. The only time I could find to lift weights at school was during my lunch period. We had a half hour to eat, so I'd gobble my lunch in five minutes and go down to the weight room for the next twenty-five. Coach Long was often in the weight room as well, and I tried asking him for help. I wanted to learn some different techniques on how to lift more effectively, more efficiently. He just brushed me off at first.

"I've got *players* to coach," he told me. "I don't have time for you. Go ask someone else."

But I kept going to the weight room. I kept lifting. I kept getting stronger. Every day, Coach Long saw me in there, working my tail off, just like I told him I would. Finally, after weeks of this, he started paying attention to me. He started helping me.

"You're not getting low enough," he'd tell me as I tried to squat 315 pounds. "Unlock your hips first and make sure you get parallel."

He encouraged me to try out for the track-and-field team that spring, and I did—not as a runner, of course, but as a discus and shot-put thrower. That May—on my birthday, actually—I won the high school state championship in discus by throwing the metal disc 149 feet on a cold, rainy, miserable day. That's about 15 feet farther than I'd *ever* thrown. To this day, I still don't know how I did it.

With that success, and with the fat that was indeed slowly melting into muscle, the Britneys of the world started looking at me a little differently. Sure, a girl did turn her nose up at me when I came straight from the weight room to the science class. (I'd worked up quite a sweat, and I'm sure I wasn't the most pleasant-smelling guy to sit next to.) But my classmates could see that I was changing.

I had just turned sixteen years old. It felt as though my whole life—my whole life in high school, anyway—was turning around.

No one was calling me Sherman anymore.

"Be Better Than Me"

The next year, I tried out for the football team, just like I told Coach Long I would, and I began to excel there. I stayed on the track team, too, competing in both discus and shot put. I eventually won state championships in both. In fact, I won the state championship in discus three times.

But sports still didn't crack my priority list. It was still *faith, family, education*. I might've been good at football. It might've helped make me more popular at school. But what happened on the football field or at a track meet took a back seat to what I did in class.

I've already said how important education was in our family and that both Ducie and Dana went to college. But my family wasn't rich, and it wasn't easy for my parents to send them. I sometimes heard my parents in heated debates over how they were going to afford all that schooling. I didn't want to put my parents through that a third time.

If there's anything that I can do to take that burden off my parents, where they don't have to worry about paying for college, I'm going to do it, I told myself. I worked far harder in the classroom than I did out on the football field because I was angling for an academic scholarship after high school. I wanted someone to pay *me* to go to college.

I wasn't even thinking about an athletic scholarship. None of my family even considered such a thing. I played football just to widen my social circles a little. For me, football wasn't about the thrill of the game or the competition or dreams of playing in the NFL. I wasn't wired for any of that. It was about being liked.

That changed one day when Coach Long suggested that academics weren't the only way a university would pay for my schooling.

"Jason, what are your goals in high school?" he asked. "What do you want to achieve here?"

No-brainer, I thought. After all, I had my list of priorities. "Academics are my first priority," I said. "I want to get good grades. I want to go to college."

"So, what about football?" he asked. "What do you want to achieve there?"

I shrugged my shoulders. "I just want to play for you and have a good time," I said. "But my academics always come first, all right? I need that scholarship."

I think he almost rolled his eyes.

"Jason, don't you know you could earn a scholarship playing football?"

Just like that, a bell went off in my head. "Seriously?" I asked. Sports were so off my family's radar that it had never occurred to me that someone might pay for me to go to college to play *sports*.

"Seriously," Coach Long said. "I think you've got a great shot at one."

That changed the trajectory of my high school career. It wasn't as if my education took a back seat to football. I still studied hard, still graduated as a member of the National Honor Society. But knowing I had two chances for a scholarship—one in football and the other in academics—made me redouble my commitment to the sport.

I gave it my all during every single practice—so much so that when practice was over, I'd have nothing left. I'd go home, take my shower, eat my dinner, and go to sleep at seven-thirty or eight. But I still had homework to do, so I'd set my alarm for three in the morning. When the alarm went off, I'd head straight for the bathroom, splash cold water on my face, and get to work.

Later in my high school career, while the rest of my classmates were socializing and goofing around during their lunch period, I'd sneak my lunch into the library and use that time as an extra study period. Out of seven hundred students, I was the only one using the library during lunch. In fact, I wasn't supposed to be eating lunch there, but it was what I had to do. I told the librarian just that after she caught me one time eating a sandwich. I promised her I'd never do it again. But the next day I was back, during lunch. I was there every lunch period after that too. She could probably tell I wasn't missing any meals, so I think we just came to an understanding. Don't ask, don't tell.

"Hey, Jason, are you coming in here to study?" she'd ask.

"Yes ma'am," I'd say.

Meanwhile, back at home, the house was filling up again. My dad had truly retired from his job in Washington, DC, when I was in high school, and Ducie was back too.

He'd gone to North Carolina Agricultural and Technical State University on an ROTC scholarship. But, as you remember, he also loved video games. Well, in college, he got around a whole bunch of other students who loved video games just as much. He washed out of school, came back home, and started picking up odd jobs here and there. He worked at a restaurant for a while. He worked at a cable company. He moved back in with my parents and started working as a guard at a nearby prison. Ducie had battled earlier with some maturity and time-management issues, and he was paying the price for that now.

Yet even if he was struggling to find his way a bit, he came into his own as a brother. Ducie knew he'd made mistakes, and he was determined to make sure I didn't make the same ones. As I was finding new success in high school, he was encouraging me in everything I did, filling me up with love and praise and advice.

"Jason, I want you to do better than me," he said. "Jason, be better than me."

He kept pushing me, kept encouraging me, kept pouring love and affirmation and support into me, like the best big brother in the world.

I wasn't losing to him anymore; he was helping me win.

College Bound

It was my junior year and we were already in the middle of track-and-field season. The team boarded the school activity bus to head out to the meet, with Coach Long doing the driving. But as I was about to board, he closed the bus door partway so I couldn't climb on.

"Jason, stop right there!" he hollered.

The rain was pouring down, splattering over my jacket and wetting my face. "Coach, it's raining," I said, as if he couldn't see that for himself. "Let me on the bus."

"No," he said. "I want you to soak in this moment. I want you to remember this moment for the rest of your life."

I wasn't thinking about soaking in the moment. I was thinking about the rain soaking into my clothes.

"I'm pretty sure I'm going to remember this, okay?" I hollered through the rain. "What is it?"

"I just got off the phone with Coach Ken Browning from the University of North Carolina at Chapel Hill," Coach Long said. "They want to offer you a full ride. A full scholarship to play for them."

I stood for a minute, the rain forgotten. "Wow. Really, Coach?"

"Yes."

"That's awesome," I said. "Can I get on the bus now?"

He opened the door and I climbed aboard, wiping water away from my face. *Wow*, I thought again. *All the weight lifting, all the practices, all the 3 a.m. mornings—they'd paid off. The University of North Carolina was going to pay my way through college.*

The Race

Happily ever after, right? My dreams, my expectations, everything I wanted to achieve in the short term had been realized. Not only did I know that I was college bound, but I had reached new levels of popularity. In my senior year, I was voted both homecoming and prom king. *Zero to hero,* they say. That was me. I was Northern Vance High School's homegrown hero. Everyone was saying so. And I listened. Boy, did I listen.

As most everyone in my life was pumping my ego up like a balloon, Ducie was trying to keep my feet on the ground. He started warning me about the dangers of thinking too much of myself.

"Jason, look, we're all proud of you," he told me, "but you need to have some humility too."

I didn't listen. Why should I? I was headed to UNC on scholarship. He'd washed out of school. I worked really hard and excelled both on the football field and in the classroom. When Ducie was my age, he worked hard and excelled at only one thing: video games. My future was limitless. He was working at a prison. His future, it seemed, was literally locked in a cage. I didn't have to put up with his love of *Star Trek* or his skill at *Mortal Kombat* anymore. My big brother wasn't beating me at everything like he used to. He wasn't beating me at *anything*.

"Be better than me," he had told me. Well, his wish came true. I *was* better than he was, or so I thought. I loved him too much to say it—up until the day we buried my grandmother.

She died in spring 2001. She had lived the latter part of her life in Washington, DC, so the whole family went up for the funeral. Not many people knew about my scholarship then, so for me the funeral served double duty: our whole extended family could remember my grandmother and celebrate my achievements at the same time.

For most of the day, that's exactly how things played out. Everyone at the funeral was praising me. I, of course, soaked it all in like a paper towel.

Ducie was getting a little tired of hearing "Great job, Jason," and "Way to go, Jason." He saw my pride. If he couldn't hold down my helium-filled ego, he was determined to prick it.

We were standing outside the church in our black suits and dress shoes. He'd heard the praise I'd gotten all day, and I was ready for more—from him, from my big brother. Instead, he turned to me and looked me in the eye.

"Jason, everything you've done is great . . . ," he started. "But you need to show a little humility in your high position."

He'd said this to me before, and I'd always smiled and nodded and completely ignored him. This time, Ducie went further. He wasn't just offering me advice; he was a little fed up with me, and he was about to let me know it.

"I'm your big brother, and you know what that means?" he said. "I'm always going to be bigger than you, faster than you, and stronger than you."

My eyes opened wide, like a cartoon character's. Ducie had obviously lost all perspective, all sense. *No way* was he bigger than I was. That was obvious. *No way* was he faster or stronger. *He* wasn't going to UNC on scholarship. I wasn't the fat tag-along kid anymore. I wasn't the little boy that Lunsford would beat so badly in video games. *Who was Ducie, pretending he was better than me?* I thought. *Hasn't he been listening to everyone else?*

I was furious. I wanted to just punch my brother in his face. Maybe he wanted to punch me too. But we were dressed in our funeral clothes. We were mourning our grandmother. We weren't going to start fighting right outside the church. We were angry, but we had enough sense and grace to stay away from anything stupid.

"You're faster and stronger than me, huh?" I told Ducie. "Really? You want to make a bet?"

The street in front of the church was an empty strip of asphalt. Many of my grandmother's mourners were slowly dispersing.

"All right, let's see who's faster," I said. "Right now."

So we took off our jackets and stepped into the street with our sharp-creased pants and dress shoes. A few family members had gathered to watch, laughing and talking a little. And sure, it might've looked as though Ducie and I were just kidding around, blowing off a little steam after sitting in that church for so long, but I wasn't just kidding.

We decided to run down fifty, maybe sixty yards—a distance familiar to me from football practice. Ducie used to play football, too, but that was years ago. Who knew how long it'd been since he had run. I figured I had the race in the bag.

"Ready . . . ," someone said.

I felt the asphalt through the soles of my shoes. Now, after all this time, I was going to put my big brother in his place, to show him who *really* needed to be humbled. After so many years of getting beat by Ducie, I was going to beat him. After spending my entire childhood following his lead, he was going to follow me for a change.

"Set . . ."

I leaned forward a little and, out of the corner of my eye, saw Ducie do the same. He might've been smiling, I don't know. I wasn't. The time had come to show him—to show my family—I wasn't the fat little baby brother anymore. I was a big man, and a big deal. I was everything my parents hoped I'd be, and I was determined to make sure everyone, including Ducie, knew it.

"Go!"

My shoes pushed against the asphalt, sending me farther, faster down the street. I could hear the sound of my soles scraping and felt the wind in my face as I saw Ducie—my layabout, video-game-loving brother Lunsford—in *front* of me. I pushed harder. I tried to run faster. It didn't matter.

Big brother beat little brother by a country mile.

I crossed the finish line, wherever it was, and bent over, hands on my knees. I was huffing and puffing like the Big Bad Wolf. Ducie walked over to me, smiling arrogantly, I thought at the time.

"Look, man, we're all proud of you," he said, "but you can be humble as well, all right? You don't have to walk around like you're the big man on campus. Like you're a big shot."

I should've listened. I should've smiled, nodded, and shaken his hand. Given him a hug. More than that, I should've *humbled myself.* Just like Ducie told me I should.

But I'd been beat. *Again.* I was hurt. Humiliated. At a time when I was finally feeling good about myself, it felt like Ducie was trying to drag me back down—put me back in a place that I'd long outgrown.

I stood up straight and stared at him, eyes as icy as I could make them. "You know what? I've got a scholarship to play football at North Carolina!" I yelled. "What are *you* doing with your life that's so great? What are you doing with your life that's so awesome?"

I waited for the angry words, for the comeback that Ducie always seemed to have at the ready. He had a quick mind and a quick wit, as skilled with comebacks as he was with pencils and paintbrushes. If someone jabbed him, he'd always have a parry ready to go.

But not today. I watched the smile fall from his face and the mirth and kindness drain from his eyes. Earlier, I'd wanted to punch him in the face. Right now, he looked like I had.

He didn't say a word. He turned and walked away.

Did I feel bad? Maybe. But I was too angry to notice, too sure of what I'd said, and too enthralled by this cheap little victory to care.

Dana, our sister, had watched the whole thing.

She said, "Jason, you're a jerk. You need to apologize."

"No," I said. "I'm not going to apologize. He doesn't deserve it." And I walked away too.

My sister was right. *Of course* she was right. Ducie was right too. I'd let my hurt and pride and arrogance take control. But sometimes I think God can use even our mistakes for His purposes. He can bring His goodness out of our badness.

A couple of months later, I noticed that Ducie was doing things differently. He was dieting. Exercising. After years of bouncing around from job to job, he was showing a focus that no one had ever seen. I didn't know why. No one in the family did—not until he made an announcement.

"I finally know what I'm going to do with my life," he said. "I'm going to dedicate my life to service. I'm going to join the United States Army."

I tried to talk him out of it at the time. I thought of him and all his talents—the beautiful pictures he drew, the work he did with stone and brick and wood. And, selfishly, I didn't want him to go. The United States wasn't sending troops to Iraq or

Afghanistan at the time, but to serve in the military is an inherently dangerous calling. Risk is part of the job.

"The military?" I said. "Why you want to do that, man? There are so many other things you can do with your life."

He looked at me, didn't even pause. "Jason, I've got to do this," he said. "Before you can help somebody else, you first have to help yourself."

He said it with such boldness, such conviction. I didn't understand what Ducie was telling me fully at the time, but I knew he meant it. I knew I couldn't talk him out of it and that I shouldn't. I had to accept Ducie's decision. I walked over to him and hugged him.

He married his fiancée, Sherrie, that fall. Two days later, he went off to basic training. After years of feeling stuck, Ducie was experiencing some massive changes, exciting changes.

I was, too, taking my scholarship offer and heading an hour's drive southwest to Chapel Hill. I was a Tar Heel now.

Losses and Lessons

The University of North Carolina is basketball country. With seven national championships and eighteen Atlantic Coast Conference titles on its ledger, how could it not be? Michael Jordan and Los Angeles Lakers legend James Worthy both played there—on the *same team,* in fact. When people think North Carolina Tar Heels, they think hoops, not the gridiron.

But when I arrived, you could sense a potential shift. The basketball program was going through a rare rough patch. Yet, in 2001—the first game I saw action in, in fact—the Tar Heels football team beat Florida State University, a program that at the time was ranked sixth in the nation. It was a first in the school's football history that North Carolina had beaten a top-ten team. After losing our first three games that season, we finished the rest of the regular season with a 7–2 record, polishing it off with a 16–10 win against Auburn in the Peach Bowl. Hopes were high for the following season.

But the team sagged my sophomore season. I moved from offensive tackle to center that year—the position that my line coach, Hal Hunter, called the line's most important position—and started all twelve games. But the team finished 3–9. Going into my junior year in 2003, I didn't see any reason to believe that the team would be much better. My life wasn't falling apart or anything. My grades were strong, and earlier in college I met the love of my life, Tay—beautiful, brilliant, ambitious Tay. I'll have much more to say about her later, but for now I can just say that from our first days together, she became my rock, and we'd known each other for just a few days when I knew, without a doubt, that she's who God wanted me to spend the rest of my life with. She and I were married in the summer of 2003.

But when you play Division I football, everything else in your life—grades, relationships, everything—must make space for the sport. Football takes an enormous amount of your time, energy, and spirit. Sure, I was doing *my* job well, according to the coaches. I was considered one of the strengths of an otherwise disappointing team. Some people were already telling me that I might be NFL material. After my college career was done, I might be playing on Sundays.

But football is a team sport. Yes, it's nice to play well. It's nice to hear your coaches praise your efforts. It's even nicer to win. I could've played a perfect game, but it didn't mean much if I headed into the locker room a loser. When you play football, you're a piece of a machine. You can be a really great piston in an engine, but if that engine doesn't turn over, it doesn't much matter. And when the season looks like it's heading south before it's even begun, you're bound to feel disproportionately gloomy too.

Ducie, meanwhile, had become a father. His daughter, Amber, was born in June 2003, while he was in Iraq. He wasn't allowed to go home to see her, but Ducie's wife, Sherrie, sent him pictures of her regularly. And every day, when he was out in the field, he'd wear a picture of his daughter on his ID band, strapped to his right arm.

That August, at the end of our long, hard football training camp, my parents came to Chapel Hill to have dinner with Tay and me. I was really looking forward to it. It was a great opportunity, I thought, to vent about everything that was going wrong with my life. If there's any shoulder that's good for crying on, it's my mama's.

Right after Tay and I climbed into the back seat of my mom and dad's vehicle before dinner, I launched into my sorrows. I recapped the team's horrible season last year. I told her that the team wasn't going to be any better this year.

"All the guys are selfish," I said. "They're just way too into themselves."

Looking back, that's pretty ironic—me pointing the finger of blame at everybody else. I was pretty full of myself in that moment, thinking I was a strong link in what I perceived to be the weak chain (my football team). My brother had cautioned me; he'd told me to be humble. *You don't have to walk around like you're the big man on campus,* he'd said.

But I *was* the big man on campus. I was setting weight-lifting records for the school. Humble? At that time, I still didn't feel I had anything to be humble about. All my problems, all my woes—I was sure they were someone else's fault. I knew that if anyone could understand that—could understand all my woes and hardships—it would be my mom. She'd make me feel better. She'd commiserate with me, reassure me, just like she'd always done. *Oh, baby, everything's going to be all right,* she'd say. *You just work hard and do your best, and that's all anybody can ask for.*

But she *didn't* say that. She just sat there, in the front seat, not uttering a word. That's not like Mom at all. She has something to say about *everything.*

So, after I went on for about ten minutes, mapping out all my sorrows and frustrations, I began to worry. *Did she fall asleep?* I wondered.

"Mama? Can you hear me? Are you listening to me?"

She hadn't fallen asleep. She wasn't thinking of just the right words to say to make me feel better.

"You need to shut up," she said, not even turning around. "You need to *shut up.*"

I was stunned. I didn't know what to say.

She wheeled around to look at me flush in the face, her eyes hard and hurt.

"Nothing you're going through in your life right now—*nothing*—can compare to what your brother's going through, fighting and serving our country in Iraq and Afghanistan," she said.

That was all she said. She turned back around and that was it. That was all she needed to say. If my ego had been a balloon—one that had gotten bigger with each passing year since I was sixteen—Mom had effectively untied the string and let all the air raspberry out. After it was completely deflated, I realized just how full of pride and selfishness I'd been. I had been thinking of only myself, when my brother—someone I loved, someone I'd respected for so much of my life—was going through trials and hardships and dangers that I could never, ever imagine.

I didn't say sorry. I didn't say anything. Nothing else needed to be said.

That before-dinner speech of my mother's, as short as it was, flipped my attitude completely around. Football suddenly got a lot easier—not physically but mentally.

Listen, playing football at a high level is never easy. I worked hard that season, as hard as ever. I lost plenty of sweat in practices and games. But my mom helped put all that work and all that I was going through into perspective. I stopped wallowing in self-pity. I started to reflect more on the elements of my life that were truly important to me—the things that meant something. If I had a bad practice, I thought about my brother in his desert camouflage, patrolling the streets of Abu Ghraib. If I lost a game, I thought about Ducie's daughter and how much he must long to see her.

The Knock

My father heard the news first. It was September 21, a Sunday. My mom was already at church for Sunday school. My dad was still at home getting ready to meet her for the service when he heard the knock.

He opened the door and saw the men in their green dress uniforms and spit-polished shoes. He knew. Before they opened their mouths, the tears welled up in his eyes.

"Y'all get off my porch!" he shouted. "Get off my property! Whatever you came here to tell me, I don't want to hear it!" He shut the door in their faces. He started weeping. He couldn't stop.

But they didn't leave.

• • •

My mom was at church, in Sunday school, when the church phone rang. "Deborah, it's your husband, Bernard."

"Hey, honey, is everything all right?"

Moments later, her fellow churchgoers watched as she fell to her knees.

. . .

We'd lost again. The day before, we'd played a road game up in Wisconsin, 38–27—our third straight defeat. But when you play Division I football, you get very little time off. That Sunday morning, I was getting ready to go back to the facility. The medical staff needed to check us out. We players needed to watch game film to see what went right, what went wrong, and how we could improve next week.

My mom called around ten-thirty, maybe eleven. It wasn't unusual for her to call, as we often talked after a game. She sounded normal enough.

"Hey, son, how're you doing?" she asked.

"Doing good, Mom."

"Are you getting ready to go back into the football facility?"

"Yes ma'am," I said.

She might've paused just a little bit before she spoke again.

"Hey, baby, I need you to do something for me. Do you have Coach Bunting's number?"

Coach John Bunting was the head coach for the Tar Heels football team my entire career at UNC. He'd recruited me. But when my mom said this, part of me wanted to roll my eyes a little. I thought at first she was kidding. See, Mom would sometimes joke around with me after a game. *You know, someone needs to talk with your coach about how you played,* she'd say. *Give him some good advice.* Every time, I'd tell her no. *Don't ever say anything to my coach,* I'd tell her. *Please don't be* that *mom, trying to tell him how to do his job.*

"Mom," I said with a touch of mock exasperation in my voice. "Why do you need my coach's number?"

Mom was still very calm, very composed, but she wasn't relenting. "Just get it for me, would you? Can you get that for me quickly? I need it as soon as possible."

"Um, sure," I said. "I'll work on it right now."

I'd just hung up when I got another call, this one from my aunt June.

"Hey, Jason," she said, sounding a little strange. "How are you doing?"

"I'm doing good, Auntie," I said, really puzzled by now.

"Good, good," she said. "Listen, have you talked with your mother?"

"I just got off the phone with her," I said. "She was just asking for my coach's phone number. What's going on, Auntie?"

"Um, no. Yeah, you just need to call back your mother."

"What's going on, Auntie?" I asked, my voice rising a little.

"Just call your mother back," Aunt June said.

After receiving my aunt's suspicious call, I knew there was a full-fledged family-wide conspiracy going on, so I called my sister in Washington, DC, but she didn't know any more than I did. By now I knew that something serious was happening, but I hadn't put together all the pieces yet. So I called my mom back.

"Did you get me the number for your coach yet?" she asked.

"No, Mom, no," I said. "What's going on? Look, Aunt June knows there's something going on. Dana knows something's going on. What's happening?"

She paused. "Son, I just need you to do what I asked you to do, all right? I need you to get me the number for Coach Bunting."

Suddenly, the truth hit me. It hit me hard. I felt it, like a bullet, in the center of my spirit.

"It's Ducie, isn't it?" I said.

She took another long pause. "Yes, baby," she finally said. "It's your brother."

Mom knew how hard the news would hit me. She knew how devastated I'd be. She wanted my coach's number to make sure I'd be safe—to arrange for travel back home to Henderson. She knew I'd never be able to see the road through my tears.

· · ·

Army Specialist Lunsford Bernard Brown II died September 20, 2003, in a mortar attack in Abu Ghraib, Iraq. He was twenty-seven years old. He left behind a loving wife, Sherrie, and a three-month-old daughter named Amber—a daughter who looked just like him, a daughter who'd never seen him in person.

I hadn't seen him myself since 2001. Two long years.

Before you can help somebody else, you first have to help yourself, he'd told me. I can still see his face as he said it. The words roll through my mind as if he is in front of me, speaking to me now.

How many prayers had we said? Between his mother and father and brother and sister and all his family and friends, how many thousands and thousands of prayers had been said on behalf of him—asking God, *begging* God, to protect my big brother? Every day. Every night. Every meal.

So many prayers, and to have that happen—to have them seemingly go unanswered—it just makes you wonder. *What's going on, God? Why?*

I made it home to Henderson safely. Coach Bunting drove Tay and me there himself. Looking back, it was a tremendous sacrifice for him. His team had just suffered a crushing loss. A game against North Carolina State was next, our biggest rival aside from Duke. He had work to do, hours upon hours of work to get ready for the next game. But he found the time to drive me home himself.

I spent the rest of that Sunday, and most of Monday, with my family. Those who've lost someone close to them can probably imagine what that time was like. You cry and wipe the tears away. And then you cry some more, wipe away more tears. And when you think you've got no tears left to shed, you cry some more. It feels like it'll never stop.

My mom encouraged me to go back to Chapel Hill—to spend time with my "other brothers," as she called them, some of whom I'd called selfish just a month or two before. I returned to school Monday night and was back at class and practice on Tuesday. I played the game against North Carolina State. The record shows we lost, 47–34, and I'll take the record's word on that. I don't remember the game. I couldn't tell you a single thing that happened that afternoon on the field. My body was there, snapping the ball and blocking, just like always. Physically, I did my job, but mentally and spiritually, I was somewhere else. I only remember red that day: the red of my opponent's jersey. Not a single snap, not a single block, not a word, not a play. Just red.

Ducie's funeral was the next day—a week after my dad told the soldiers to get off his porch, a week after my mom collapsed to her knees. Two charter buses brought the whole football team—all the players, the entire coaching staff—from Chapel Hill.

Many coaches talk about how a football team is "family." Most of the time it's just that: talk. Spend a little time with the coaches, with the players, and you see that their character is far away from that idea of family. But when I saw all my teammates file into church—right after a loss to North Carolina State, right when they should've been breaking down game film and preparing for the next opponent—I knew it wasn't just talk with this team, or with Coach Bunting. I remember looking into the eyes of every single one of my teammates that day. They shed just as many tears as I did.

And guess what? Every single one of those tears they shed was like one less tear that I had to shed myself.

The apostle Paul wrote in Galatians 6:2, "Bear one another's burdens, and so fulfill the law of Christ." That day, my teammates were carrying my burdens. They were carrying my pain. They were there for me, at the lowest point of my life.

Sometimes people will ask me if I miss football. Every time, the answer is the same: *No*. But the friendships? The camaraderie? I do miss that. I treasure the memories of those times and the friendships I still have. My mom called them my other brothers, and she was right. They're my brothers. They're my family.

Tagged

The mortar round came right through Ducie's tent. It hit the table right where he was standing. Ducie was the closest to the blast; his body absorbed most of the shrapnel, and by being where he was, he saved lives. Ducie died, but the soldiers who stood behind him lived.

The blast was so strong that it tore through both his dog tags, right where his heart was. Sherrie kept one of those dog tags, the one that was most intact. But she gave me the other one—the one with the clear and obvious hole in it. The hole's near the bottom, right where his middle initial is stamped. The hole's jagged. It's sharp.

I wore that dog tag around my neck every practice, every game, for the rest of my college career. I turned the jagged side in so I could feel the metal wound. When I put on my tight shoulder pads, when I pulled on my fitted jersey, I could feel the tag press into my skin, into my chest.

That was my reminder. *Jason, you have nothing to complain about,* that pain told me. *Jason, you have nothing to feel sorry about. There's no pain you can feel, no pain you can experience, that compares to what your brother sacrificed.*

Not everyone knew I was wearing it. But every hit I took, every block I threw, I'd feel Ducie's tag dig into me a little more—prick me where it counted.

That pain, strangely, made me *joyful.*

It gets hot in Chapel Hill. Practices can go for two or three hours at a time. You're working and running and hitting and falling. Sometimes all the work and effort and contact and especially the heat can feel unbearable.

While my teammates complained, I walked around with a smile on my face. "Come on, guys!" I'd holler. "Come on, let's push a little harder!"

See, the pain of practice was nothing, *nothing,* compared to the pain near my heart. It was the thorn in my flesh.

In 2 Corinthians 12:7–8, Paul wrote about his own thorn. He asked—"pleaded," according to some versions—for God to take it away. But God said no. "My grace is sufficient for you," God told him, "for my power is made perfect in weakness" (verse 9). In verse 10, Paul said that he was glad for the reminder: "I am content with weaknesses, insults, hardships, persecutions, and calamities. For when I am weak, then I am strong."

That dog tag reminds me of my weakness. It reminds me that we're *all* weak—that life itself can be fleeting and, to our mortal eyes, far too short.

But it reminds me, too, of the strength we find in God—that in our own weaknesses, His strength is made manifest. That when we live in Him and follow Him, we can be "content" with whatever comes our way. A three-hour practice in ninety-degree weather isn't enough to rob us of that contentment. Of that joy.

I don't know why Ducie was taken from us. I still miss him. I will never stop missing him. I don't know why God allowed what happened to happen.

But I do know that my brother lived a full life, a life worthy of honor and praise. The *whys* of what happened never go away. But the *gratitude*—the joy that he was with us for as long as he was, and the understanding that while here, he made lives better—comes back. We may cry because our loved ones are gone, but we can smile because they were here. That they impacted our own lives. That they helped shape us and mold us for the better. We have hope that we'll see them again someday.

Sometimes, by way of an icebreaker, people will ask what three people someone would most like to eat dinner with. If someone asked me, I wouldn't name a football player; I wouldn't name a celebrity. I'd want to share a meal with Jesus. With Grandpa Jasper. With my brother. Those three lived well. They fought the good fight of faith and finished their race. That's what I want to do as well: Fight the good fight. Finish the race. Live a life of purpose.

CHAPTER 4

Faith, Family, and . . . Fortune?

God calls us all for something. He calls us to be fathers and mothers, doctors and teachers, leaders and servants. He calls a few to be football players too.

For a while, I was one of them.

He gave me all the gifts I needed to play football. Ever since high school, I'd had the size to play on the offensive line—the physical presence to fill a gap. After years of lifting, I developed the strength not just to fill that hole but also make my presence known there. I could protect my quarterback from charging nose tackles and make gaps through the defense for a running back. I had the ability to play the position mentally, as well—a job that, according to ESPN's Adam Rittenberg, often makes centers the smartest people on the team. The position requires much more than just snapping the football and pushing around another guy like a sumo wrestler. You've got to know—or figure out fast—what every one of the twenty-two players on the field are about to do, adjusting line coverage and spotting potential trouble on the fly. And you've got to do it all while the quarterback might be calling his own audible and barking out the snap count.

If I had been a pretty good player before, Ducie's dog tag gave me the extra push to the next level.

The tag reminded me that whatever faced me out on the football field was nothing compared to what Ducie went through. Whatever sacrifices I made for the team, it was nothing compared to Ducie's own. I didn't feel like I was playing with just his dog tag; a little bit of Ducie was with me. It gave me drive and a never-say-quit attitude. And my teammates saw it.

"Jason, what's wrong with you?" they'd say on a ninety-five-degree day while I was cheering them on. "Are you immune? Are you a machine?"

I was a man on a mission. That constant reminder of Ducie made football *easy.*

Don't get me wrong: The sport is difficult. It demands a lot. But for the rest of my career at Carolina, I knew that no obstacle was too difficult, no challenge too hard. I was a match for pretty much anyone on the other side of the line, and if I ever *did* get beat on a play—if a defensive lineman ever got the best of me and knocked me to the ground—I'd bounce back and shake it off quickly. They say that quarterbacks need to have short memories; the same can be said of offensive linemen. Every once in a while, even the best get beat. The secret to being the best? To shake it off and get right back in the game—body, mind, and heart.

Playing on the line, I was never going to get the broad recognition from the fans that quarterbacks or wide receivers or star pass rushers do. Offensive linemen are rarely destined for stardom. But the coaches knew. My teammates knew. The opposing teams knew. I developed the reputation of being one tough son of a gun.

Jason Brown is tough, they'd say. *Jason Brown has no quit in him.* I was the guy you wanted to go to football battle with, the guy you wanted beside you. I strove to be that guy. After all, that's the kind of man Ducie was—a man who would, and did, literally lay down his life for others. And, although I knew that football was a game, that nothing I did on my field of battle could be remotely compared with what Ducie did on his, I was determined to emulate my big brother—to be the sort of man he pushed me to be.

Having Tay by my side didn't hurt either.

Glowing

When you look at medieval or Renaissance paintings of Jesus or Mary or the saints, they often have halos around their heads—bright disks of yellow or gold radiating from their faces like a sun. It was the painter's way of encouraging the viewer to look more closely at the man or woman and remember the saint's role in God's story. *This person,* the painter tells us, *is special. This person is walking with God. See him. Notice him. Behold him.*

Now, I'm not saying that Tay's a saint. But when I first saw her, she was glowing. No joke.

Let me back up for a minute.

When I first arrived at UNC, I was ready for a serious relationship. At first I was determined to find that relationship the right way. I prayed to God to send me the right person. I prayed and I prayed and I prayed. I promised God that I would abstain from any sort of sexual immorality—to be pure and save the gift of physical intimacy for only my wife. I said, *God, I'm going to leave it all in Your hands.*

But I also put Him on a timetable. And instead of me waiting for God to show me the right person, I thought I'd give Him a helping hand. I saw some cute girls running around on campus and thought that maybe God had chosen one of them for me, and me for her. I was trying to force God to pick someone *I* wanted Him to pick.

God wasn't having any of that. Every time I approached one of these young women and asked her out to dinner or a movie, she would turn me down flat. It wasn't "Sorry, Jason, the time's not right." It wasn't "Can we just be friends?" It was just the straight-up, flat-out "Get lost" sort of rejection. After a couple of months of this, I was getting pretty discouraged.

Meanwhile, I was watching some of my more womanizing teammates have the time of their lives. It's not that hard to be a ladies' man when you're part of the football team, and those guys made the most of it. My route of staying pure and trusting God was getting me nowhere in the relationship department. God was not working fast enough for me. So I decided to take the matter into my own hands. When a few of those friends invited me to a little hole-in-the-wall club in Durham, North Carolina—home to Duke University and just a half hour from Chapel Hill—in late April 2002, I decided to go and try it their way for a change. I went to the club with the worst of intentions.

My intentions that night fit right in. The nightclub was not what you'd call a real classy establishment. It was the sort of place that changed its name every couple of years after a fight or a shooting or something, and it was filled with plenty of people who also had the worst of intentions. I had already gotten three phone numbers from three different women when I looked across the room and saw Tay. I could tell right away that she was different—very, very different—from anyone I'd danced with that evening. She was dancing with a few of her friends, and she was absolutely luminous. Not figuratively: *literally* luminous. There was, truly, a glow about her. Maybe it was a trick of the club's lighting, but it seemed God was making sure I noticed her—pointing the equivalent of a big neon arrow at her. *Behold, Jason.*

So I walked up to her and used what must've sounded like the corniest pickup line ever.

"Girl . . . you're glowing."

"Excuse me?" Tay said with a wrinkle of her nose. "What did you just say?"

"You're *glowing*," I repeated.

We introduced ourselves. I asked her if she wanted something to drink.

"I don't drink," she said with a frown. Strike one. (I learned later that she never went to nightclubs, either. She was there that night only so that one of her best friends wouldn't have to be there alone.)

"Oh, no, no," I said, trying to recover. "I didn't mean *alcohol*. Of *course* not alcohol. I meant, can I get you some water?"

We talked for the rest of the evening in a quiet corner of the club. I could see from the very beginning how much we had in common—how important faith was to her, how smart and determined she was to succeed without ever losing track of God in her life. When closing time came and everyone started pushing for the door, I had Tay hold on to the back of my shirt and walk behind me while I used my offensive-line skills to clear a way to the parking lot. There, I showed her my 1999 Chevrolet Tahoe, which I hoped would impress her.

It didn't. Strike two.

I asked her for her phone number.

"No," Tay said, and my heart sank. Glow or no, neon sign or no, it felt like I'd struck out again.

"I'm not giving you my number," Tay repeated, "but I'll take yours. And *I'll* call *you*. *Maybe*."

Tay

When people meet Tay today, they think she's the quietest, most introverted, most loving person they'd ever met. And she is.

But they don't see the lion.

She reminds me a little of Jesus in that respect: the lion and the lamb. Everyone wants to choose the lamb side of Jesus. They want to see Him as being so meek and mild and loving and, of course, being our best friend. No one wants to talk about the lion side of Jesus—the guy who turned over the tables in the temple market or said in Matthew 10:34, "I have not come to bring peace, but a sword." When Jesus comes back, He's coming back as the Lion of Judah, and we better watch out. He's not playing around.

So many people see only one side of Tay. They see only the lamb. My children and I know about the lion—that fight she has inside her. She needed that fight growing up.

Some people might think that because Tay graduated from Duke University, one of the country's most elite and most expensive colleges, she must've been born wealthy. But it's just the opposite. Tay grew up south of San Francisco, in the San Mateo/Palo Alto area. Her mother was just seventeen when she had Tay, and for a long while it was just the two of them, trying to figure out how to make it in a hard world.

Tay and her mom weren't wealthy people. They didn't have

a car. They didn't have a washer and dryer, and Tay remembers walking block after block with her mother, carrying their clothes to the laundromat. They'd walk to the grocery store, then walk back carrying bags and bags of food through some very bad neighborhoods.

But God was with them—both Tay and her mom believed that. Her mother taught her valuable lessons and instilled character inside that little girl with every step through those neighborhoods. She taught her to fight. To never give up. To never make excuses.

Back then, Tay and her mom fought for everything they had, and they always, praise God, had food on the table. But those lessons stuck with Tay. They stuck with her through high school, where she fought like crazy to succeed and excel. They stuck with her as she worked to raise money for college and applied for scholarships. They stuck when she made her way into Duke, where she had a job straight through college to pay for tuition as she made her way through dental school. She worked and fought for everything she's achieved. She's a lion, through and through.

Maybe it was only fitting that she'd make me fight for her too.

• • •

The day after Tay and I met at that dive in Durham, she called me and we arranged to go out to dinner that Saturday. The afternoon of the date, I threw away all the trash in the Tahoe and bought a single white rose for Tay, which impressed her way more than the Tahoe did. I had hoped to take her to what qualified as a pretty fancy place for a couple of college kids: Outback Steakhouse. But the hostess told us there'd be a two-hour wait for a table, so we went right next door and ate at

Bob Evans instead—a chain that sells and serves down-home comfort food like country-fried steak and pot roast. It was just a humble country meal, but it was *real*. And that made it a pretty fitting first date with Tay.

The very next day, I called my parents.

"It's over," I said. "I've found the one. God sent me the woman I'm going to marry."

And He had.

We dated for about fifteen months and got married on July 25, 2003. We were both still in college. I was just twenty years old.

Ducie died less than two months later.

Looking back, it feels like Tay came into my life at a crucial time. If I hadn't had her support in the days right after Ducie's death, I'm not sure what I would've done, what bad choices I might've made. The tragedy shook me to my very core. I thought about quitting school. I contemplated quitting football. When I lost my brother, a big part of my foundation was knocked out from under me. But Tay, along with my parents, gave me another foundation to rely on—another source of comfort and support when I needed it more than anything in my life.

Over the next couple of years, that foundation grew bigger and stronger. When God chose Tay for me, He chose well.

We were completely compatible in every way, it seemed: We loved God. We both wanted between three and five kids. She was finishing up her own degree when we met, preparing for dental school, and she was smart and driven, just like I was. We both dreamed big, and we were focused on achieving those dreams and ambitions. We didn't have time to party. We didn't have time to goof around much. But when we got married, even though we were both working really hard, we saw each other every day. Everything felt normal. Like that Bob Evans meal, it felt *real*.

But as my graduation inched closer, and as the NFL draft drew nearer, our shared future was going to be challenged in some unprecedented ways. During those years in college, we'd shared the same priorities that I'd embraced way back in middle school: faith, family, and education. But now our future was on the threshold, knocking at our door. And it didn't just come with a big cardboard Publishers Clearing House–like check; it came with some new demands too.

Decisions, Decisions

For most careers, college graduates can choose, within reason, where they'll be employed. They can apply to the businesses and corporations they'd most like to work for, ignoring those they'd rather not. They might only send résumés to the cities or towns where they'd want to live. They might get multiple offers, and they can choose the one that seems to them the best: the best money, the best location, the best fit for them and their families.

It works differently for draft-worthy NFL-bound football players. There've been a few exceptions, but for the most part, the National Football League *tells* you where you're going to work. And that can make planning for the future, especially when you're newly married, a little more difficult. I knew that once I was drafted, I could be heading to any one of thirty-two teams located in every possible area of the country. I might be heading to Boston or Miami or Seattle. And if Tay and I were just concentrating on *my* career, we could relocate together.

But as hard as I'd been working in the sport of football, Tay had been working hard to reach her own goals in the field of dentistry. As excited as my family and friends were for my opportunity, her family and friends were just as excited about her future. Her family had sacrificed a lot to help send her to Duke, and they had hopes and dreams for Tay. She needed to apply to dental schools well before I knew where I'd be playing professional football.

Both of us knew from the first night we met that we each had big goals. We knew how serious we were about those goals. After all, we'd spent the past two years watching each other work like crazy to achieve them. We knew what our priorities were: We valued our faith. We loved each other. We wanted to start a family and pour all the care and attention we could into our children. Neither of us was trying to pursue selfish goals without thinking of the other.

But those opportunities—those dreams we had that we'd sacrificed so much for—were calling us. And our families, our friends, the whole *world* would think we'd be absolutely nuts if we ignored that call.

By the world's logic, the decision we made was a good one—the best possible one. We decided to keep our home base in North Carolina. I'd go wherever the draft took me. Tay would apply for dental school at UNC. She'd become a Tar Heel, just like me. And we'd just be sure to make our relationship work around our careers.

One of my teammates, Ronald Brewer (we called him Brew), asked me what team I wanted to go to. I told him, hands down, that it would be awesome if I were to be drafted by the Carolina Panthers. They're my home-state team, after all, located right down in Charlotte and just a couple of hours away from most everything I'd ever known.

Brew asked, "So is that what you're praying for?"

"No," I said. "I'm just praying for God's will to be done."

"Come on, Jason," Brew said. A committed Christian, he quickly broke out Scripture, quoting from Psalm 37:4: "The Word says, 'Delight yourself in the LORD, and he will give you the desires of your heart.'"

I had to explain to Brew that just because I *desired* to play for the Panthers at the time, it didn't necessarily make them the best fit for me, my family, or my career. Only God knew what the right fit would be. I didn't have a crystal ball. I couldn't see the future. I wanted the decision to be where it belonged: in God's hands, not my own.

Drafted

By my senior year at North Carolina, all the experts said I was one of those surefire NFL players. Most of them, including ESPN's draft guru Mel Kiper, said I was almost guaranteed to be a "first-day" guy, meaning that I'd be drafted in one of the draft's first three rounds. Friends and family encouraged me to throw a party on that "first day," a Saturday, so that we could all celebrate my success together.

Yeah, I'd heard that before. But I didn't want to celebrate too soon. I'd seen other guys throw first-day parties only to end up feeling discouraged or even humiliated when they weren't drafted until later or not at all. Not to mention how uncomfortable it was for those of us at the party!

So, instead of throwing a party, I went fishing. Tay and I went to my parents' house in Henderson that day, where they have a small pond in their backyard. While my mom watched the draft on TV, I brought out a lounge chair, set it up right by the pond, and took a nap. I slept right through *not* getting drafted. And I was very much at peace about not being picked.

The next day, during the fourth round, I got a call from Ozzie Newsome, the general manager for the Baltimore Ravens at the time.

"Hey, Jason," he said. "We're on the clock, and we just wanted to know if you would love to come and be a Baltimore Raven."

"Daggone right, I would!" I said. "Thank you very much."

I wasn't lying to Mr. Newsome. Baltimore was a great fit for me—better, I think, than Carolina would've been. God always knows what He's doing, doesn't He? And it was still close. Only two teams, Carolina and Washington, were closer to Henderson and my parents' backyard pool. I was just a five-hour drive away from the Ravens' training facilities.

And although it's always gratifying for your ego to be drafted early, my agent (Harold Lewis, of the National Sports Agency) said that being drafted in the fourth round was the best thing that could've happened to me. Based on the NFL's bargaining agreement with the player's union at the time, first-round players were locked into five- and six-year deals. That sounds good on the surface; I originally wanted to sign as long a deal as possible, because a longer contract equals more security. But, as Harold pointed out to me, it also locks players into lower wages for a longer period of time. That same bargaining agreement limited the amount teams could pay their draft picks too.

As a fourth-round pick, the Ravens wanted to give me only a three-year contract. In the fourth year, I'd be a restricted free agent (which meant that I could talk with other teams but the Ravens could match any contract offer and keep me). And in the fifth year, I'd be an unrestricted free agent, which meant I'd be free to sign with any team I wanted to.

"I know how good of a player you are," Harold told me. "You're going to outperform your rookie contract. And because you'll hit free agency sooner than the players drafted ahead of you, you're going to be able to break the bank that much faster."

So now I knew where I was headed and where I'd be working, God willing, for at least the next three years: Baltimore.

I was drafted by the Ravens about the same time Tay was accepted by UNC. That meant we were going to be separated— live physically apart for much of the year and try to make a long-distance relationship work as best we could. It was the sort of concession I think many couples in our position would make. When the American Dream calls, you answer. You *must* answer, people say. *Do you know how many people would kill to be in your position?* they'll tell you. *How many people would give their lives for that opportunity you have right now? If you have an opportunity to climb that corporate ladder, to make a boatload of money, to be a professional athlete, then you better do it.*

So you start shifting your priorities around. You start making those calculations. You start compromising.

God's math is always different from our own. He's a jealous God, and when we start compromising—when we make that American Dream our priority instead of following Him—we fall out of alignment. We forget our priorities. We lose our center.

When I was growing up, my mom must've said a thousand times, "You can't have your cake and eat it too." I never knew what that meant. If there's a piece of cake right in front of me and I eat it, sure, it's not in front of me anymore. But I still have the satisfaction of eating it, right?

But my mom knew what she was talking about. You can't have everything, even if the world tells you that you can. Every choice comes with a cost. And sometimes the cost can be pretty high.

Rook

I was rich. I was heading to play for a franchise that, just a few years before, had won a Super Bowl. And I won't lie: I was excited about it all. My hard work and dedication had paid off. I was going to play professional football, a vocation that millions would envy. But even then, I was worried about the implications.

The NFL season starts around the middle of July, when training camp begins. The Baltimore Ravens held their own training camp back then at McDaniel College, located in a Baltimore suburb called Westminster. Now, if you know anything about that area of the country, you know how hot and muggy it gets in summer. It can be miserable to even step outside, much less spend hours in that heat, running up and down in full pads. The humidity is so terrible that ESPN even did a story on it one year. It's even hard to breathe in weather like that. The air just presses down on your shoulders and sometimes feels as though it might suffocate you.

We weren't the only ones out there in that heat. Ravens fans are true fanatics. Thousands would show up to watch us practice, suffering through all that heat and humidity just to have a chance to say hi or get an autograph. So, naturally, players are encouraged to shake a few hands and sign a few autographs when practice is done.

I was a rookie offensive lineman. No one was spending hours in the heat to see me. Fans wanted to talk with Jamal Lewis, who two years before ran for 295 yards in a single game, or Todd Heap, a two-time Pro Bowl tight end called the Stormin' Mormon. They wanted to see Jonathan Ogden and Ed Reed, who both have since been inducted into the Pro Football Hall of Fame, or Deion Sanders, another Hall of Fame legend, who was finishing out his career in Baltimore. And they *especially* wanted to see linebacker Ray Lewis, perhaps the greatest linebacker to ever play the game.

These were some of the NFL's biggest heroes. Football gods. I was just a fourth-round draft pick. And that gave me time to look around a little.

One afternoon while we were over at one end of the field where all the fans gathered to meet the players, I looked over across the field to the other side. There I saw a man standing all by himself. I could barely see him through all the humidity. There was a haze blanketing the practice field, and it made me wonder whether I was seeing him at all. So I turned more fully toward him and put my hand to my forehead, trying to shield my eyes from the glare of the sun, just trying to make out who or what I was seeing.

And then I knew: it was Jesus.

I heard Him speaking to me—not across the field, but in my heart.

Who is going to follow Me? He asked. *Who is going to follow Me?*

I know there'll be doubters out there. Maybe I was a little hazy myself because of the heat. Maybe the image was just some fan who got lost. Skeptics could figure out a thousand different ways to brush that moment away.

But I know what I saw. And I realized, in that moment, what a challenge God had given me. He'd brought me into a game, a profession, that is surrounded with rampant idolatry. I heard those fans holler for autographs, and I knew that for many of them, those players—those Baltimore Ravens—were their *idols.* They'd wear their jerseys. They'd hang up posters in their bedrooms and man caves. They'd scream on Sundays for the players to save the game. For a few fans, a player like Ray Lewis might as well walk on water.

I thought about all the children who grew up watching those

games, who grew up loving their favorite players. Just because I was a Baltimore Raven—because I wore the jersey and played on that green field—I was, in a way, idolized too. I was no Ray Lewis, but I *was* a Raven. And I remembered what Matthew 18:6 said about those little children: "Whoever causes one of these little ones who believe in me to sin, it would be better for him to have a great millstone fastened around his neck and to be drowned in the depth of the sea."

That plagued me for a while, because I was a little guilty of idolatry too.

Ray Lewis might be one of the most passionate football players I've ever met. Every game day, Ray would watch the movie *Gladiator* on a portable DVD player as he got ready for the game. As Russell Crowe's gladiator Maximus Decimus Meridius suited up, so would Ray. As Maximus fired himself up to enter the arena, so would Ray. They both got ready for battle—to entertain the masses with their sweat and blood.

It was hard to look at Ray Lewis—at the time a two-time Defensive Player of the Year and Super Bowl MVP—and not idolize him a little. My rookie year, that was the guy I was going to have to face at almost every practice. It was kind of intimidating.

Then one day while we were in the locker room, a light bulb went off for me. I saw Ray putting on his armor, just like I did. He put on his socks, and I put on my socks. He put on his jockstrap, and I put on my jockstrap. He had to lace up his shoes the same way that I had to lace up mine. Underneath all that armor, he was a man. Just like everybody else.

Most people see their superheroes only in uniform. We don't see them when they're vulnerable. But I did. I saw Ray when he got treatment for all the bruises he'd suffered on game day. I saw him in the cold tub from being so sore. And, for me, that leveled the playing field.

He's just a man, I thought to myself. *Just like I am.*

The next day at practice, the coach called a play where I was supposed to go to the next level—and that meant squaring off against Ray Lewis.

And I pancaked him. I didn't just block him. I knocked him down and fell on top of him, eliminating him from the play.

We got back to the huddle, and Tony Pashos—a third-year offensive tackle and a good friend of mine on the team—pulled me in.

"Jason," he said, "what did you just do?"

"I just did my job; that's what I did."

"No," he said. "No. You don't do that."

"What do you mean, 'You don't do that'?" I asked.

"You don't pancake Ray Lewis," Tony told me, showing a wisdom beyond his youth.

I was still puzzling over this when the next play was called— the very same play that we'd run just a minute before. I'd need to face Ray again.

I came through to the next level, getting ready to block Ray. But then, an instant before I could get my hands on him, he somehow juked to the side, grabbed the tail end of my jersey from my back, and pulled it over my helmet. And then he threw me to the ground. *Hard.*

So there I was, my arms flopping around like stalks of grain in a strong breeze. I couldn't see anything because the tail of my jersey was covering my eyes. I flailed around like a 320-pound fish on the riverbank. And when I finally freed myself of the jersey, I saw Ray staring at me with a look that Maximus Meridius himself would've been proud of.

He didn't say a word, but his eyes said, *Rook, show some respect.*

I didn't say a word. But my eyes said, *Yes sir.*

Ray Lewis was just a man. He still is. But even men deserve a level of honor too.

New Lives

After a rough 2005, my rookie season, we won thirteen regular-season games in 2006, losing just three. It was the best regular-season record in the franchise's history, a mark that wouldn't be topped until 2019.

My career was beginning to click. Although the travel was tough and the time we spent apart from each other painful, Tay and I were trying to do the best we could under the circumstances. I spent as much time at home in North Carolina as I could during the off-season (roughly February through July). It was far harder for me to get back during the football season, but I drove home as often as I could. Whenever Tay had a break, she tried to drive up to Baltimore to see me. But you just can't get much quality time in those short, unreliable visits.

But we were both excited to welcome a third member of our family.

The Ravens had just finished playing in Buffalo, New York, on October 21. It was the last game before our bye week, which meant that I had almost a week of rest and recuperation time before the team would start formally preparing for our November 5 game against the Pittsburgh Steelers. I was looking forward to spending that week with my very pregnant wife. As soon as the team got back to Baltimore, I made the five-hour drive down to North Carolina. I didn't even tell her I was coming back home that night.

When I pulled into the driveway, her car wasn't there. No lights in the house were on. She wasn't answering her phone.

In desperation, I called Tay's best friend to find out what was going on.

"Oh, *hey,* Jason," she said sweetly. "I'm with Tay. In the hospital."

Tay had gone into labor that morning. She didn't tell me because she didn't want to distract me from the game.

Think football players are tough? They don't have anything on my wife.

Two days later, JW came into the world. I call him my first-begotten son.

With JW's arrival, I wanted to be home even more. But the NFL doesn't give paternity leave. We finished out our 5–11 season that year, then went 11–5 the following year. But to be part of that successful season, I was doing something I promised myself I would never do.

You remember my daddy issues: I knew what it was like to grow up without a father in the house. I knew what it was like to see my dad just every now and then. He sacrificed his *time* with us to *provide* for us. His job in DC allowed us to buy a slightly nicer house, to drive slightly better cars, to afford a few luxuries. But back then, when I was missing him so much, I didn't care about any of those things. You can't put a price tag on the time you spend with your father.

And here I was, doing exactly what my dad had done. I was a great provider, but I knew in my heart that I wasn't being a great father.

About a year after JW was born, and at the beginning of that successful 2008 season, I was preparing to leave for Baltimore again. Tay was still working her way through dental school, and I'd just dropped JW off at the babysitter's house, just like I'd done countless times. I said goodbye, just like I'd done countless times. But somehow my son—even though he couldn't even walk yet—knew that this goodbye was different. As soon as I put him down, he was *bawling*—wailing as loud as he could with those little baby lungs of his. He was clawing at my legs. He was crying so hard that he couldn't even get out the word *no*, but I knew what he was saying to me.

Daddy, don't leave me, he was saying. *Please don't leave me.*

But I did. It tore my heart out, but I turned and walked away. I didn't stop. I didn't stay. And in that moment, I felt like I had abandoned my child.

When I tell that story, some people think I'm laying it on a little thick. *Oh, that's so dramatic,* they tell me. They remind me that this experience isn't unique. Many mothers and fathers work. Lots of children spend much of their time with babysitters or at day-care centers. People go to work every single day and sacrifice that time so their families can have bread on the table and clothes on their backs.

Just like my father did. Just like I was doing.

I get why both parents work, why they leave their children with babysitters and day-care centers and preschool. I really do. But man, when I look at the state of families today—all the brokenness experienced in so many homes—I believe it's often because our priorities aren't where they're supposed to be. Look at the shattered families, the divorce rates, the rise in anxiety and depression in kids. Is it because we, as parents, sometimes focus on the wrong things? That we focus on the worldly treasure, and we overlook the priceless, living gifts that God has given us? Does anything—even an NFL career, even a Super Bowl ring—compare with a great day with our children? Does a seven-figure bank account outweigh the time we could spend with our kids playing catch or fishing or just talking? I don't think so.

Breaking the Bank

My NFL career was shaping up just like my agent said it would. I started all sixteen games at center in 2008, that 11–5 campaign, and I helped turn Baltimore into one of the league's top rushing offenses. We went to the playoffs again, ultimately losing to the Steelers in the AFC Championship Game. We were one game away from the Super Bowl, but by any measure, we had a successful season. I still had that reputation of being one tough son of a gun, a guy without an ounce of quit in him. And as I went into free agency, I was considered the top interior offensive lineman available.

The St. Louis Rams, a team that had gone 5–27 the previous two years, were looking for some heavyweight help, and they turned to me. The Rams pulled out their checkbook and signed me to a five-year, $37.5 million contract, making me the highest-paid center in NFL history at that time. I was the team's first pickup—the first piece to what new head coach Steve Spagnuolo hoped would be a successful rebuilding effort.

"There was no question he was going to be the guy we were going to focus on at that position," Coach Spagnuolo told the Associated Press after I signed. "I'm just glad it all fell in place like it did."

Tay finished dental school the same year I wrapped up my time in Baltimore. It freed us both up to move to St. Louis, to build a real home. No more commuting back and forth between cities. And although the life of an NFL player is never normal, it looked as though we were getting closer to some semblance of normalcy. I'd come home from a day at the "office" and spend the evening with my wife and son. It wasn't *The Brady Bunch,* maybe, but I hoped that we were on the way to feeling like a family—a real family.

Looking back, I don't think our priorities were right on target. We were going to be a family on *our* terms. Like the great philosopher the Notorious B.I.G. once said, "Mo money, mo problems."

Every strong family needs a place to live—a family home—so we bought a house: a ridiculous twelve-thousand-square-foot mansion with marble fireplaces and exotic wood floors and two massive bars. We didn't drink, but it didn't matter. I stocked those bars with every high-shelf bottle of liquor available, right down to a $1,500 crystal bottle of Louis XIII cognac.

When I wasn't playing football, we also went to church every week, putting on our best clothes and heading off to the service, just like a good family is supposed to do. We looked the part of the perfect American family on Sunday mornings— a perfect power couple with their adorable little boy. But Monday through Saturday, our lives were anything but perfect.

Everything looked like it had fallen into place for us, but Tay and I weren't clicking the way we used to. The time apart had taken a toll on our relationship, and we lost the humility and grace we used to give each other. We were prideful, arrogant.

I was a big, important football player. Everyone was telling me how great I was. But Tay didn't see it. Why couldn't she see how wonderful I was? Why couldn't she see what everyone else saw in me? Meanwhile, Tay—*Dr.* Brown now—was ready to be respected as well, and she wanted me to *show* her that respect. And if I didn't show it sufficiently? There'd be problems. We were fighting all the time, it seemed. We felt out of sync.

We'd pursued our dreams. We'd reached our goals. We'd achieved everything we'd worked so hard to achieve when we were poor, happy college students. But our success—all the wealth and fame and respect we thought would make everything great—actually made it harder to live with each other. Individually, we'd done everything we'd wanted to do. But our marriage, our family, was hurting. And no one knew it but us.

Faith and family, we'd always said. *Faith and family.* Those were supposed to be our priorities. I think we still paid lip service to them. But our actions? Our attitudes? Our pride? Anyone who looked closely at our lives could see that our real priorities were different.

Man in the Mirror

It was May 5, 2010. My birthday. I woke up in our mansion, pushed the thousand-thread-count sheets off my body, put my feet on the exotic wood floor, and shuffled off to the bathroom. I should've been happy. I turned twenty-seven that day, and it seemed as though I'd already given myself every worldly gift possible. My presents were all around me.

But I found myself thinking about Ducie. He was twenty-seven years old when he died. I thought about what I'd done in my life and what he'd done. I realized I couldn't compare the two. I was playing a *game* for a living. I was in the entertainment business, giving people three hours of distraction on a Sunday afternoon. Ducie had lived a life of service.

People always told me that I looked a lot like my brother, especially when we smiled. But when I looked at our lives—how we lived them, what those lives said about our values and priorities—I realized they didn't look much alike at all.

I looked in the mirror. And I saw Ducie.

You know what that reflection told me? The same thing that bratty, snotty-nosed kid had told Ducie years before, right after losing a race.

What are you doing with your life that's so great? the reflection said. *What are you doing with your life that's so awesome?*

I knew in my spirit what the answer was: *nothing.*

. . .

"Keep your eye on the ball." Almost every coach in almost every sport says that. For most athletes, it's rule number one. But in football, that feels especially true, even when the ball isn't actually moving. In the moment before the snap, every eye is focused on that football. Every offensive player is listening for the quarterback to call for the snap. Every defensive player is focused on that ball, waiting for it to move out of the center's hands. Every man, woman, and child watching the game—be it a field of three hundred or a stadium filled with eighty thousand—is waiting, almost breathlessly, for the ball to move.

All the action centers on that weird-shaped, blown-up piece of pigskin. I guess it makes sense that the guy who sets it all in motion, every snap, would be called the center. He is, in a way, the center of that tiny, self-contained world of sport at that moment, in the pause before the storm.

Maybe I took my role of center too seriously. For the next several years, I listened to the world. I became the center of my own existence. I had my mansion. I had my eight-figure NFL contract. I had what the world says to value. And, ironically, I'd taken my eye off the ball.

"Do not love the world or the things in the world," the Bible says in 1 John 2:15–17. "If anyone loves the world, the love of the Father is not in him. For all that is in the world—the desires of the flesh and the desires of the eyes and pride of life—is not from the Father but is from the world. And the world is passing away along with its desires, but whoever does the will of God abides forever."

It was time to get back to the basics. It was time to find the ball again. That scolding in the mirror, Ducie glaring back at me in my own reflection, planted the first seed of what would be a whole new direction in my life.

But as every farmer knows, it takes a while before you see that seed start to grow.

CHAPTER 5

A Different Sort of Field Goal

I'd been humbled in my reflection. Ducie, almost seven years after he died, had challenged me like he always had. *Be better than me,* he'd tell me when I was in high school. Well, I didn't think I could ever be better than Ducie, but I could be better than *me.* Better than the me I'd been the past few years.

But how? You don't walk away from an NFL career. *No one* does that. Even if I did, what was I going to do that was better?

Naomi, our second child, was born in May 2011, but by that time our family was crumbling fast. Tay and I did a great job of sticking on smiles for the outside world, and everyone thought we were a model couple—loving, successful, faithful. We were playing the tune the world wanted to hear. But we knew that we were playing it while the ship was going down, like the violinists on the *Titanic.* Tay knew what kind of man I really was. She knew how selfish I was. She knew what a hypocrite I was. She'd had enough. By late 2011, Tay was researching divorce lawyers and drafting separation papers. I just hadn't been served yet.

Day by day, week by week, our relationship had grown weaker and weaker. Our slights turned into fights and became more and more frequent until Tay and I were barely speaking to each other. There wasn't necessarily a single moment, but just the wear and tear of a partnership when the partners aren't in sync. Marriage is supposed to be about *we,* but somehow for both Tay and me, it became all about *me.*

The NFL is hard on relationships. Every professional sport is, if you look at the statistics. According to the *New York Times* and *Sports Illustrated,* the divorce rate for pro athletes ranges between 60 and 80 percent—much higher than the national average. Everyone thought that Tay and I would be the exception, but we weren't.

My marriage wasn't the only thing falling apart. The career that I had sacrificed so much for took a bad turn too. The Rams were in the middle of a miserable season in 2011 (we'd go on to finish 2–14 that year), and when you're losing that often, those in charge are willing to try anything to turn the season around. Everyone's job is on the line, especially for the coaches. Late that year, Coach Spagnuolo, the same man who made me the centerpiece of his free-agency pickups just a couple of years before, called me into his office and demoted me. I was no longer the Rams' starting center.

I'd been a backup before, but never in my football career— not in high school, not in college, not in the pros—had I cracked the starting lineup and then been benched. I was devastated.

I went into football as a business decision. I didn't grow up loving the sport, and I don't even watch much of it now. But football had been so good to me, and I had been so good *at* it, that I'd put the sport on a pedestal. I'd turned it into an idol—the source for not just my wealth but my happiness too. My identity and self-esteem were wrapped up in football.

Again, "do not love the world or the things in the world." My first love was supposed to be God, but somewhere along the way, I'd fallen in love with football. And football wasn't loving me back anymore.

I was failing as a father too. I'd come home from work exhausted, both physically and mentally. Many times, I didn't give my family the best because I'd already given my all to the Rams. I knew I wasn't the father I could've or should've been, but I saw that particularly clearly around Christmas of that year.

Now, we Browns aren't big on Santa Claus. We hadn't stuffed JW's head with visions of sugarplums that Christmas. But Tay and I barely saw him enough to stuff his head with *anything*. I was away most of the day. Tay was working full time as a dentist. We'd drop JW and Naomi off at a day-care center around six-thirty or seven in the morning, and sometimes we wouldn't pick them up until six at night. In an average day, we could count on one hand the hours we spent with our children. We were handing our kids off to strangers, and those strangers were the ones teaching them.

One night near Christmas, I came home completely exhausted. I'd been working with the backups and the practice squad. I was angry because I knew I should be starting. I was frustrated to be working so hard and still be sidelined during the game. The last thing I wanted to do that evening was turn around and be a good, attentive father.

But four-year-old JW wasn't having it. He had a job to do.

"Dad! Dad!" he said. "We gotta go outside!"

"Son, I don't want to go outside," I said. "I'm really tired, and it's really cold."

"But we *have* to," JW whined. "We've got to feed the reindeer! They'll never make it around the world if we don't!"

I noticed that JW was holding a little Ziploc bag filled with Chex Mix and pretzels and sprinkles. *Reindeer food,* according to his day-care center.

I didn't want JW thinking about reindeer on Christmas Eve. I didn't want him thinking about a bearded old elf handing out gifts. I wanted him to think about the *real* gift of the season—to remember that, as the book of James says, "Every good gift and every perfect gift is from above" (1:17). Feeding these mythical reindeer and leaving cookies out for Santa Claus felt like idolatry. I wanted him to know that the only jolly fat man eating cookies in *our* house on Christmas Eve was going to be *me.*

I sat him down, and we started talking about the difference between what was real and what was pretend.

"Son, is Spider-Man real or is he make-believe?" I asked. Spider-Man was pretty popular then, and JW had seen some cartoons starring the superhero.

JW thought for a second. "Make-believe," he said. He'd seen drawings before. He knew the difference between a drawing and a real-life person.

"Is Iron Man real?" I asked. This was trickier because, unlike the cartoon Spider-Man, Robert Downey Jr.'s Iron Man sure *looked* real on screen. JW said, "Iron Man's *real.*"

"I'm sorry, son," I said gently. "Iron Man's not real."

We went through all his favorite superheroes, some he thought were real and some he knew weren't. We finally got to Santa Claus, and I broke the news to him: Santa isn't real either.

But then I asked one final question, the million-dollar one: "JW, is *Jesus* real?"

JW thought about it, and thought about it hard.

"No, Dad," he said. "Jesus isn't real. Jesus is make-believe."

That's when I knew I was failing my son. I was failing my family. Tay and I were so engulfed in the things of this world, we weren't teaching our children about the things that mattered most. We were chasing success and fame and money—things that, compared to God's greatness and His gifts, might as well be make-believe too. It wasn't just JW who couldn't tell the difference between what was real and what was imaginary. I was guilty of that too.

Faith and family, I'd always said. *Above all else, faith and family*. But I hadn't taught my family about my faith. Not enough.

Down the Drain

Not long after, I had what I can only describe as a vision. I was in our home's great room when Jesus painted me a picture of my future so clear, so vivid, that it felt like it was in high definition. He showed me in that house all alone. That huge mansion was empty, except for me. He showed me the brokenness of myself. He showed me the crushing loneliness I felt. Not only were Tay and I divorced, but I also wasn't even able to see my children or hold them or tell them that I loved them. In my vision, they were nowhere around—not even in the same state.

In that vision, I saw my brokenness. It literally brought me to my knees.

All my life, I've wanted to be in control. And for the most part I had been. I took control of my life in high school and never looked back. I worked hard to drive my own destiny. I sacrificed so much to build the opportunities I'd built. I'd been able to control everything—to *fix* everything—in my life.

Until now.

My marriage was broken. My family was broken. My life was broken.

I was the strongest player ever to come through North Carolina; I could squat more than eight hundred pounds. But I wasn't strong enough to fix this. I graduated from one of the best universities in the country, but I wasn't smart enough to fix this.

This was the last position I ever wanted to be in. But you know what? It was exactly the position Jesus wanted me to be in: a position of complete surrender, complete humility, complete obedience.

"Jesus," I said, tears running down my face, "whatever You want me to do right now, I will do it. I know that You can restore and redeem my family. I know that You can restore and redeem my marriage. Jesus, that's what You're best at. That's what You do. I know that I can't do it, but I know that You can. Whatever You want me to do, I will do it."

Jesus responded to me in a clear audible voice: "POUR IT ALL DOWN THE DRAIN."

I wrinkled my brow. *That's kind of cryptic,* I thought. *What does that mean? I said I will do whatever You want me to do.*

"POUR IT ALL DOWN THE DRAIN," He said again.

I was still on my knees, but I turned my head around and looked at the liquor bar behind me. I saw all those bottles of top-notch alcohol lining the shelves, liquor I didn't even drink. Then I thought about the symbolism of all those bottles—how instead of lifting the name of Jesus up in our home, we'd been enshrining the names of Captain Morgan and Jack Daniel.

"Pour it all down the drain," the voice had said. This was a start.

I started uncorking and unscrewing every bottle at the bar: gin, whiskey, brandy, vodka. I poured it straight down into the sink and watched it drain away. After I was done with that bar's stash of alcohol, I went into the basement and dumped the top-shelf liquor out of that one, too, including that $1,500 bottle of Louis XIII cognac. The walnut-colored liquid melted away in the sink, temporarily increasing the value of the St. Louis sewer system.

Tay, who could barely stand to look at me at the time, heard the clanging of all those bottles and clomped down the stairs from the bedroom.

"What are you doing?" she asked.

I looked at her, my eyes red from crying, snot coming down my face. "I'm pouring it all down the drain," I said.

"Why are you doing *that*?"

"Because Jesus told me to."

I watched as her face changed. The anger and exasperation fell away, replaced by a look of utter, complete confusion. She had never seen me like this. I was a big, strong football player. I could control my emotions. I didn't show fear to anyone. But now, for the first time, she saw a different me: someone trying to obey a higher power. It caught her completely off guard.

I'd like to say that our relationship changed right then, that all the wounds we'd given each other had been miraculously healed. It wasn't like that. She just turned around and walked away. But I'd surprised her. I showed her something she hadn't seen from me in a long time. *Humility. Submission.* In that moment, a moment that might've looked crazy to most anyone else, I was once again putting faith and family first.

In the days and weeks that followed, Tay could see that my change of heart wasn't a momentary thing—that pouring the liquor down the drain wasn't just an expensive and temporary moment of conviction after which I'd slide right back into the same patterns. She could see a change in me. She could see that I'd been humbled, that I was serious about following God's call, and that I wanted to lead our family to a better place. As she saw that transformation take hold in me, her heart began to change a little bit too. She was willing to show me a bit more grace, be a bit more tolerant of my faults.

It wasn't an easy transition. And it sure wasn't easy to ignore the world around us—the world that told us that everything we had and everything we'd done for ourselves was *great* and that for anyone to say otherwise—even if that *anyone* was us—was wrong. But Tay and I began to have some difficult conversations about what we really *did* value and what we really *should*. As time went on, I started unpacking what I thought we needed to do.

"We've got to get back to our real priorities," I told her. "*Faith and family*. Whatever comes after that, it comes after. Never again are we going to make decisions for our family based on money. Never again are we going to make decisions for our family based on the almighty dollar. We can't do that."

"So what does that mean?" Tay asked.

"I don't know exactly. It might mean *a lot* of things," I said. "It might mean that one of us will stop working."

"So who's going to stop working?" she challenged. "I spent four years in dental school. Are you going to quit football and be a househusband? Do the grocery shopping? Take the kids to school?"

"I don't know," I admitted. "Maybe. We're going to pray about it."

But I didn't know how.

Solid Foods

I'd been calling myself a Christian my whole life. I'd gone to church since the time I was a baby, and I'd rarely missed a service. I praised the Lord. I read the Bible. But now, at the age of

twenty-eight, I knew that even though I claimed to be a follower of Christ, I'd never stopped being a baby in the faith. I
was still, as Paul told the Corinthians, drinking spiritual milk.
I wasn't eating solid food (see 1 Corinthians 3:2).

I was a really good football player. I was really, really good
at being successful in the world. But I was not a good Christian.

So, how do you become one? If you've done church all your
life and it's still not enough, what do you do?

I thought back to my time in high school—how I trans-
formed from an overweight kid into a football player. I'd
trained and sweated and lifted and studied until I became one.
I'd worked my tail off to get to that point. Every goal I've had,
every dream I've achieved, didn't come from dreaming or hoping. It came about through effort. Desire translated into time
and energy.

So, when I wanted to deepen my relationship with God, I
knew what it would take: time and energy. I needed to work
at it.

I called it my spiritual training camp. The training wasn't as
physically grueling as what your typical NFL training camp
puts you through. But mentally? Spiritually? It was a workout.
It consisted of three things: fasting, praying, and reading the
Bible. Over and over. Fasting, praying, reading the Word. I
didn't even know how to pray, so I bought a book of prayers
and read those prayers over and over again. After a while, I'd
ad-lib a bit—deviate just a little and try to say some more or-
ganic prayers—but those written ones were my staples for a
long time. I'd read them aloud. I'd even record me reciting
some of the longer ones on my iPod. When we'd all leave the
house for an hour or two, I'd play those prayers over a loud-
speaker while we were gone. And when we came home, you
could sense the difference, as if our St. Louis mansion had

been cleaned and detoxed of some of its worldliness. It was as if our home, through those long iPod prayers of mine, had been anointed.

Reading the Bible was a different challenge.

I had been reading Scripture all my life, but now I was reading with a purpose, with a desire to move closer to its Author. And you know what? That Author was moving closer to me too. As I read, I felt as if God was pushing my attention to a particular story in Genesis. I'd try to move on. I'd read the Psalms or the Gospels for a while. But God seemed determined to point my attention to that very first book and the story of Joseph (see Genesis 37–50).

You're probably familiar with the story, but just in case: Jacob, a wealthy farmer and shepherd who lived in the land of Canaan, had twelve sons, but his favorite was Joseph. Joseph's brothers were jealous of him, so they sold him into slavery and he was carted off to Egypt. There, through what the Bible calls the "favor of God" and a series of wild circumstances, he became the Pharaoh's right-hand man. Joseph helped prepare Egypt for an upcoming famine, and when his brothers came to Egypt begging for food, he revealed himself to them. "Do not be distressed or angry with yourselves because you sold me here, for God sent me before you to preserve life," he told his brothers in Genesis 45:5.

Every time I read that passage, I thought, *All right, God, thanks.* And then I'd read something else. But God would pull my attention right back to that story. And finally it hit me that God was trying to tell me something very specific: *Jason, there's going to be a famine,* He seemed to be telling me. *You need to prepare.*

So I, in all my worldly wisdom, thought I knew *exactly* what to do: I ran to Sam's Club and bought canned goods and non-perishable food items and stuffed them in my pantry.

My family and I were now prepared for the zombie apocalypse.

But that wasn't what God was telling me to do at all. And He was pretty angry about it.

He spoke to me, just like Jesus spoke to Simon Peter (see John 21:15–19).

Jason, do you love Me?

"You know I love You, God."

Okay, I want you to feed My sheep. Jason, do you love Me?

"You know I do."

I want you to take care of My people.

But what did that mean? I knew He was asking more of me than just to buy food for the hungry, though I certainly had the means. He wanted more from me than to open up a grocery store.

After I'd been told to pour it all down the drain, I'd been willing to do anything for God. I was *begging* Him to send me out like a prophet or disciple of old. *I'll cure the sick. I'll raise the dead. I'll risk shipwrecks and stonings. Just tell me what to do, God.*

But as I worked through the reasoning, I suddenly saw what God was truly calling me to do—what outrageous, ludicrous, crazy path He was ready to set me out on.

"Hold on a second, God," I said. "You want me to be a *farmer?*"

Orchestrating the Exit

Yep, God wanted me to be a farmer. But Tay didn't know. The kids didn't know. And the NFL sure didn't know. I still had two years left on my contract with the St. Louis Rams. I might not be a starter anymore, but my team was counting on me.

And if I walked away from my contract—a contract that was still making me a very, very rich man—I'd have to deal with lots of questions. If I quit football to become a farmer, most folks would think I had lost my mind.

So I asked the Lord for some help.

"God, I know You want me to farm," I said. "You know I have two years left on my contract. Show me what to do. I know this is selfish, but make the transition easy for me. If You do that, I'll farm for You."

That was late 2011. On January 2, 2012—after that miserable 2–14 season—Coach Spagnuolo was fired. Less than two weeks later, the organization hired Jeff Fisher as the next head coach, inheriting a team that'd lost sixty-five games in five seasons and had very little money through which to bring in free agents to improve the team.

When a new coach comes in at the NFL level, he tends to clean house. He wants *his* coaches, *his* staff, *his* players. And he might've wondered how many players he could bring in if he got rid of my record-setting contract.

A few weeks later, my agent called me.

"Jason, I want to prepare you for this," he said, assuming I'd take the news hard. "Jeff Fisher and his staff are thinking about releasing a lot of the team's veterans, and you might be getting a phone call."

"Really?" I said. *Praise God,* I thought.

"Hey, listen, Harold, don't worry about it," I said. "If they release me, it's pretty likely that I'll hang up my football cleats and retire."

The call from the coach came a few days later. I thanked him for the call and hung up. I wasn't upset or worried or angry. Not in the least. In fact, I was thrilled. Jeff Fisher in his entire career has probably never fired somebody so happy to be fired.

I was free to pursue what God was calling me to do in a way that, to the outside world, would look completely rational. I didn't have to quit and walk away. I didn't have to answer awkward questions about why I'd give up a multimillion-dollar career to be a farmer. I didn't have to worry about people calling me crazy. I was *cut*. It happens all the time in the NFL. Many players retire shortly thereafter. Some players go on to new, unexpected careers. Chicago Bears linebacker Brian Urlacher went into acting. New England Patriots cornerback Ty Law opened a trampoline park. Former Patriots quarterback Drew Bledsoe started a winery. When Coach Fisher let me go, he took my job, but he gave me control of my own narrative. To the outside world, it would look as though I naturally just gravitated toward farming, following in my grandfather's footsteps.

It was time to tell Tay my crazy idea about—

Ring!

It was my agent, Harold.

"Jason, I know you're thinking about leaving the NFL, but you can't."

"I can't?" I said.

"No, you can't."

"Why not?"

"There are three teams that want to sign you to a long-term deal *right now*."

Despite my prayer, God wasn't going to make this easy.

Temptation

I didn't care what Harold said. I was done playing football. I didn't want to freeze to death in Buffalo or Green Bay. I didn't want to melt in Miami or sign a contract with the Denver

Broncos and spend the next several seasons gasping for air. Only a handful of teams would've made me pause even the slightest.

"Three teams, huh?" I said. "Which three?"

And when he named the three, I paused. They were the top three teams—the *only* three teams—that I would've loved to have been a part of.

"The Carolina Panthers," Harold said.

I was a Carolina boy, born and raised. My family, my history, my roots in the region go as deep as a white oak tree's. I thought back to my conversation with Brew when I was preparing for the draft: the Panthers were my dream team. And if I signed with them, my parents could go to every game. They'd be thrilled.

"The 49ers," he said.

The 49ers are located in one of the most beautiful cities in the country: San Francisco. The weather is mild all year round. More importantly, Tay had grown up in the San Francisco Bay Area. I might be a mama's boy, I might like to stay close to family, but Tay's a mama's girl and she'd always wanted to relocate to be closer to her own family. "Jason, if you ever get an opportunity to play in the Bay Area," she'd told me numerous times, "if you ever get an opportunity to play for Oakland or San Francisco, *you take it.*"

My agent said the third team: "The Ravens."

The Rams had pulled me away from the Baltimore Ravens with their huge free-agent contract. I would've loved to have stayed in Baltimore. If they would've matched or come close to the money the Rams offered me in 2009, I would've stayed. I got my start there and had my first real professional success playing for the Ravens. Wouldn't it be great to finish my career there? For many professionals, that'd be a dream.

I was determined to follow God's will, and I knew that what

He willed was for me to be a farmer. Part of me—a selfish part—tried to convince myself that maybe playing football for a while longer would fit in God's plan too. *God, maybe I can play just a few more years. Make just a little more money. Then I can go to North Carolina and be a farmer, just like You want me to be.* Hey, maybe I *could* have my cake and eat it too!

Deep down, I knew that wasn't what God wanted. He'd already made His will known to me, clear as day.

That didn't stop me from considering those other possibilities.

"You're Not Supposed to Be Here"

JW and I flew into Charlotte to visit with the Carolina Panthers first. My parents met us at the airport, and I knew that signing with Carolina would make them the happiest mom and dad in the world.

At the hotel, Mom could see that I was troubled.

"Is everything all right?" she asked.

I wasn't ready to tell her that God was calling me to a different career—that he was asking me to scrap football for farming. I couldn't tell her that even this visit felt like a sin, as I was ignoring God's will to follow my own.

"Yeah, Mom, everything's fine," I said evasively, trying to pacify her. "I just want to make the right decision."

The visit went better than I could've ever hoped (unfortunately). The Panthers' offensive-line coach, John Matsko, was my o-line coach in Baltimore, and I liked and respected him. I checked out the weight room and the training facilities, and they were all top notch. The Panthers finished 6–10 in 2011, but rookie quarterback Cam Newton looked like a star in the making—the sort of star who could lead a team to the Super

Bowl. (He did just that four years later.) Head Coach Ron Rivera, heading into his second year, had a reputation of being a player's coach.

But when I walked up to Coach Rivera—an ex-linebacker and a huge man in his own right—and shook his hand, something weird happened.

"YOU'RE NOT SUPPOSED TO BE HERE."

If you're curious as to what the voice of the Holy Spirit sounded like, it was a deep, rumbling bass. It was so real that I looked over my shoulder to see where it was coming from.

And then I realized that Coach Rivera was talking.

"So, we can go upstairs and work out a deal right now," he said. "You ready?"

The voice of the Holy Spirit was still echoing in my head, like the reverberations of a huge bell.

"Umm, no," I said. "I need just a little time to, you know, think about it. And, umm, I'm gonna have to go."

I was out of there quick.

When I met my parents afterward, they looked so excited. They figured their son had signed a new contract. My football-loving mom had the biggest smile on her face—a smile full of anticipation.

"Are we going to be Carolina Panthers?" she asked.

"No, Mom," I said. "I didn't sign a contract."

I've seen my mom look more disappointed in her life only once before: when she caught me stealing when I was fourteen years old.

No one wants to see that sort of look on his mother's face.

I was making decisions about my career, my future. But she and my dad had an emotional stake in that future too. All parents have dreams for their children. They want their kids to be happy and successful and secure. The NFL, with all its money and fame, offered plenty of success and security. To turn my back on that—well, who could blame my parents for being disappointed?

I spent so much of my life playing the people-pleaser game. As much as I wanted to make my parents happy, I saw that desire to please people as a trap, something the world, not God, tells us we should do. That's true even when it comes to family and friends, those people who love you and want only the best for you. You want to see them happy. You want to give them joy. But at the end of the day, there's only one opinion that matters, and that's God's. Not my mother's, not my father's, not my wife's. God's.

Thy will be done, not mine.

The Holy Spirit made His wishes clear. I was done with visits. The 49ers and Ravens would just have to find someone else to play on their offensive lines. I knew what I had to do now.

But even if my dreams had taken a new turn, my agent was still on the same NFL road.

Shortly after my visit to the Carolina Panthers facilities, Tay and I went to San Francisco—not to visit with the 49ers, but to visit Tay's parents. Soon after we arrived, I received an unexpected call.

"Hey, Jason," the voice said. "I hear you're in town."

It was Greg Roman, the offensive coordinator for the 49ers—and the assistant o-line coach for the Ravens when I played for them.

Greg barreled on before I could say much. "Listen, I'm just getting back into town myself, and I'd like to have you see our facilities, man—see if we can't work out a deal."

I hemmed and hawed a little. "Well, Greg, I don't know if I'll have the chance," I said. "I'm out here to spend time with my family."

Tay heard. Tay knew full well who I was talking to. "Oh, I'll watch the kids," she said with a knowing smile. What she *meant* was, *You need to meet with the 49ers because this is something that I've wanted for a long time and, if you sign, you'll make me the happiest wife in the world.*

So, I agreed to meet with Greg, and when I arrived, he told me everything I wanted to hear—every trigger word that might get me to become a 49er.

You could be a part of something special here. You'll be one of the team leaders. We're about to build a new billion-dollar stadium. You'll be playing in the best arena the NFL has to offer.

It didn't matter. As Greg was telling me all this, another voice was talking to me too.

You're not supposed to be here.

I got back to the hotel, and Tay was primed for good news. *Tell me the words I want to hear,* her look told me. *Tell me you signed a contract. Tell me that I'm the happiest wife in the world.*

I shook my head. "I'm sorry," I said. "I'm not going to be playing for the 49ers."

The smile vanished. Now Tay was angry.

"So what's the deal, Jason?" she asked. "You turned down the Panthers. You turned down the 49ers. You don't even want to *visit* the Ravens. Those were the *three teams* you said you wanted to play for! If you're not going to play football, what are you going to do?"

I took a deep breath and I spilled it.

"Dear, God is telling me that we need to sell our home in St. Louis and move back to North Carolina," I said. "He's telling me to purchase some land there. God is telling me that . . . He's telling me that . . . He wants me to be a farmer."

Stony silence.

"What?" Tay said finally. Then she slipped into sarcasm. "Jason, I'm *so happy* God is sharing all these things with you, because He's not sharing *any* of this with me!"

I understood how hard it must've been for Tay to hear me talk about farming. I knew that this was as unexpected as getting struck by lightning—and maybe, at first, just as painful. But I knew, I *knew,* that this is what God wanted for me. For *us.* And so I poured it all out. I told her everything that God had laid on my heart—every crazy calling. I told her about Ducie, about Joseph, about everything, about how God was healing our marriage, about how He was redeeming our family, about how He wanted me—us—to serve people in a very real, very tangible way.

I want you to feed My sheep. God told me this. I knew my football-playing days were done. I was being called to a different field.

New Playbook

Tay sat there and listened to me. She listened to it all. She didn't buy into the whole dream, not right then. But she received much of what I had to say with grace and an open heart. She believed I'd heard a call from God. She knew how much I'd changed in the last several months: from a selfish, inconsiderate football player to a man who was trying to follow God as well as he could. She saw the work that God was doing in my life. As for the rest? Well, she was willing to trust God, and trust me.

She took a leap of faith for me. She wasn't completely sold, and I didn't blame her. What a huge change I was asking her to commit to—to turn our backs on the comfortable lives we'd lived, the success and wealth we'd gathered, and dive into a new, strange life, embracing a career neither of us knew much about. It was a scary step for both of us. But I had an advantage: I knew that this next step was being orchestrated by God. I knew that He would pave the way for us. Tay wasn't in on those conversations. She just had to take my word for it—the word of someone whom, just months before, she was ready to divorce. It must've been terrifying.

But the vows she took in 2003—to love, honor, and obey—weren't just words. They were a solemn promise. And in that moment, what must've been one of the hardest moments of our marriage, she chose to embrace that promise. She had a faith like Paul's, a faith that could move mountains.

People sometimes ask why I didn't just start a charity, like normal rich people do: use my position as a football player to draw attention to the problem of hunger; use my money to buy food for the people who need it.

But that's missing the point. God didn't call us to throw money at the problem. He called me to be a farmer. He called me to this unique ministry. In that, I'm able to find peace and joy where I could not find those things before.

"The foolishness of God is wiser than men, and the weakness of God is stronger than men," 1 Corinthians 1:25 says. To the world, the leap that Tay and I made might've looked foolish. It might have looked just as crazy as David trusting a slingshot when facing a giant (see 1 Samuel 17:48–50), or as crazy as Moses trusting in a plague of locusts, or as crazy as a bunch of fishermen dropping their nets to follow a strange man with a strange message (see Matthew 4:18–22).

For years, I'd tried to do everything through my own strength, my own power, my own understanding of how the world worked. What had it gotten me? A broken marriage. A broken family. A broken life. The world's wisdom told me I was a success. I knew it was a lie. I was a lie. I'd built a career on spray-painted grass and artificial turf. God told me to dig deeper, to sink my hands deep into the earth and pull goodness out of it. Then He told me to pass that goodness on.

God had been trying to reach me through the story of Joseph, which He brought me back to again and again. *Jason, I haven't been blessing you this whole time so that My blessings could stop* at *you; I've been blessing you so that My blessings could flow* through *you.*

I could see how true that was and how far I'd messed up His blessings.

The most famous passage in the Bible is probably the twenty-third psalm, which begins with the line "The LORD is my shepherd; I shall not want" (KJV). Everybody loves it when, in verse 5, it talks about how our "cup runneth over." And as Christians, we often feel how true that is. Every single one of us is a cup. Every single one of us is a vessel that God pours into, and that goodness spills onto the people around us.

But in my life, when my own cup started to overflow, I'd say, "Hold on a second, God," and grab a bowl. When that started running over, I'd say, "Hold on a second," and grab a pitcher. And then a bucket. And then a barrel. I didn't want to lose a drop of God's blessings. I wanted them all to myself. I didn't want those blessings to spill into other people's lives, into a wider world thirsty for God. Those were *my* blessings. *Mine.*

But God had been working in me. That wasn't the way blessings are supposed to work.

It was time to let that cup runneth over. It was time to let those blessings flow.

CHAPTER 6

The Farm

When I was a child, I dreamed. I dreamed of a white farmhouse with a white picket fence. When I was in my early teens, when my motives were purer and God sometimes seemed closer, I dreamed I lived there. I visited that beautiful farmhouse only when my eyes were closed, but I knew it well. I knew it by sight.

In May 2012, I wasn't the same boy I was back all those years before. I'd grown up, gotten married, and played football. I'd lost my way and found it again. Tay and I were looking for tracts of land in North Carolina now, looking for a place to begin a new chapter, to follow God's call. That old dream was so far in the recesses of my mind that I'd almost forgotten it. But as we rode through Carolina's beautiful farm country with a real estate agent, looking for a perfect place to start our *new* dream, I saw it: a white farmhouse with a white picket fence. Then I saw what surrounded it: the green fields and ponds and picture-perfect barns.

I turned to Tay and said, "That's the most beautiful place I've ever seen."

In my mind, another word came.

Home.

The farm wasn't for sale. We were on the way to look at another property. But as we drove on, past the fields and ponds and picket fence, I said a silent prayer.

God, I hope You bless us with a place just like that.

First Fruits

Tay and I were going to buy a farm—that much we knew. We were going to sell our mansion in St. Louis and use the money to buy a big plot of land where we could grow food—not cotton, like many southern farms specialize in. Not tobacco, which made North Carolina famous and powered its economy for so many decades. Not industrial corn that is used to make ethanol. *Food.* Produce that you can actually pull out of the ground and pick from the trees and put on your table and eat. We knew that growing actual food wasn't going to make us rich like those cash crops might. But we weren't getting into farming to get rich. (At the time, we were already rich anyway.) We were following God.

We already knew what we were going to name it: First Fruits Farm.

The term *firstfruits* is mentioned thirty times in the King James Bible. It refers to what followers of God—the farmers and the fruit growers and the bakers—were supposed to give to the Almighty. We read in Proverbs 3:9–10, "Honor the LORD with your wealth and with the firstfruits of all your produce; then your barns will be filled with plenty, and your vats will be bursting with wine." In Nehemiah 10:35, we're told to "bring the firstfruits of our ground and the firstfruits of all fruit of every tree, year by year, to the house of the LORD." The Bible later extends that to the followers of God themselves. "Of his own will he brought us forth by the word of truth, that we should be a kind of firstfruits of his creatures," James 1:18 reads.

Tay and I used those verses as the basis for our new covenant with God. Whatever land God would give us we'd use to grow food. And we would give away the first fruits of that land—the first and the best—to people in need.

We needed to cover many steps before those first fruits could be realized, though. And the first step was to find the necessary acreage.

Under normal circumstances, we never would've even seen the farm, which we later learned was called informally (and, ironically, given my first thoughts when I saw it) the Home Place. We were on our way to see a completely different farm— an eleven-hundred-acre property available at a good price. But the straightest route to that farm had been closed. A bridge was down, and construction workers would spend most of the summer building another one. So, we went the long way around—right past the Home Place, that picture-perfect farm.

It wasn't for sale. But once I got a glimpse of the Home Place, with the farmhouse that had looked so much like the one I'd dreamed about, no other place could compare.

Still, Tay and I tried to get excited about somewhere else.

Real estate agents always talk about location, location, location, and the property we were going to see was in a great one: the Triangle area of North Carolina, between the cities of Raleigh (the state's capital and home to North Carolina State University), Durham (where Tay's alma mater, Duke University, is located), and Chapel Hill (where I had played college football). Because of its central location, most of the land in that triangle had been subdivided or broken up into smaller parcels long ago. To find a thousand acres there? Almost unheard of. Of all the properties we'd planned to investigate, this place—more than a thousand acres in an unbeatable location and at an affordable price—was the one Tay and I were most excited to see.

But we learned why the land was so inexpensive. Much of it was unusable. Quite a bit of it was floodplains. It would take a lot of work and loads of money to turn it into a good, functioning farm. If we bought the property, we wouldn't have much cash to improve it.

We drove away, knowing we probably hadn't found our farm yet. We weren't crossing it off our list, but Tay and I thought we could find a property that better suited us.

On the way back to Durham, we passed the Home Place again. Once more, I said the same prayer: *Bless us with a place just like that.* I was sinning, I knew. *Thou shalt not covet,* the Bible says. But I admit it: I was coveting thy neighbor's farm.

We flew out to see that big piece of land—the one we were technically considering—two more times. Tay and I felt that we owed it to ourselves to give the place the best possible chance. On paper, it seemed like just what we were looking for. But when we looked at it, both of us were underwhelmed.

Every time we went to see it, we drove by the Home Place. And each time we went by, I said the same prayer.

Finally, on our third visit to the sprawling farm—a visit I know the agent was sure would be the clincher—we told him no.

"This place, it just isn't right for us," I said. "We're just going to have to look at some other properties."

I'm sure the agent must've been disappointed. When you take a client to look at a property three times, you're bound to close a sale, right? But he didn't show his disappointment. He went to an unexpected plan B.

"I know you want a place around here," he said. "I know you're qualified. Listen, there's another tract of land nearby that you might be interested in checking out. It's not for sale, but I think the owner would be willing to entertain some offers."

Tay and I looked at each other and shrugged. "Sure, why not?" I said. "Where is it?"

"Actually, you might've noticed it on our way up here. It's the big farm with the rolling hills. The ponds. The white farmhouse. Do you know the place I'm talking about?"

"Yeaaahh," I said, trying to keep a straight face. "Yeah, I think I know the farm."

This time, instead of driving past the Home Place and praying, we pulled into the driveway. Instead of looking at those barns and ponds from the road, we saw them up close. What I told Tay before seemed even truer now: it *was* the most beautiful place I'd ever seen. We drove across all eleven hundred acres of it, and every inch *fit*. The silos were framed against the North Carolina sky. The water in the main pond rippled gently. I could hear birds sing in the trees, frogs grumble in the rushes. I tried to keep my poker face, but internally I was absolutely giddy.

Then I learned how much the owners wanted for the place. Beauty like this, apparently, doesn't come cheap. They wanted twice as much as we could pay. We'd never be able to get close to the asking price. It felt as if God might've been playing with us—showing us the perfect place before snatching it away.

We made an offer anyway—much lower than the asking price. Their counteroffer came down a little from their original price. Our counteroffer came up a little. I could see the pattern: if we met in the middle, like we were heading, it'd be far, *far* more than we could afford.

Tay loved the place as much as I did. But I knew I'd have to break the news to her: the Home Place, as much as it felt like home to us, wasn't going to land in our laps.

"They're not coming down far enough or fast enough," I told her. "I'm sorry. I know we prayed about this, but we're going to have to look somewhere else for land."

And then Tay did something utterly unexpected: she challenged me. The woman who I dragged into this crazy dream of mine, who had wanted me to play football for another few years, who'd given up the pay and prestige of being a full-time dentist to follow her husband into a world she and I knew nothing about, looked me straight in the face and stared me down.

"Jason Brown," she said, eyes flashing. "Where's this man of faith, this man of God, this man who claims that God led him away from the NFL to be a farmer and feed his people? Where's your faith now, Jason Brown? Huh? Where's your faith *now*?"

Man, she said it with such conviction and with such force that I got all teary eyed.

"Yeah!" I said, blubbering a little. "Where *is* my faith?" I didn't know if God intended this farm for us. But I knew that He wanted us to be farmers. I knew that where our resources were limited, God's were without limit. He could move mountains. He could drain oceans. If God meant for this to be First Fruits Farm, He would make it so.

I took a big black Sharpie pen and on the offer sheet wrote a dollar figure that brushed close to the very limit of what Tay and I could afford—and still much less than what they were asking. Next to the number, I wrote, "FINAL OFFER!" Then I underlined those two words. We knew it was a long shot, but we submitted the bid in faith. God's will be done.

We waited patiently for a response, and finally our real estate agent called.

"If you can close in thirty days, the farm is yours."

Moving Mountains and Millionaires

I didn't know it then, but the farm had another suitor—one with a lot more zeros at the end of his bank account.

North Carolina has its share of relatively small family farms and huge commercial operations. Much of the land here is owned by wealthy, largely absentee, owners. When I say *wealthy,* I'm not talking about *retired–NFL lineman* wealthy. These "gentlemen farmers" have a net worth in the hundreds of millions, or even the billions. They're not typically interested in using the farms they buy as *farms.* They don't want to raise crops or tend livestock themselves; they simply want to add the land to their portfolios and to have a place where they can go and do some hunting and fishing. They don't want to work the land; they want to play on it. The eleven-hundred-acre parcel we looked at three times? The place that we *didn't* want? That's owned by a billionaire now.

I understand why those big-dollar "farmers" are drawn to the land around here. Many farms like ours almost serve as wildlife refuges too. They can be home to deer and turkeys, raccoons and foxes, otters and even bald eagles. All sorts of fish populate the ponds. I don't think there's anything more beautiful than a North Carolina farm. Our farm has, I'm told, some of the best wildlife, best fishing, and best views to be found anywhere in the state. In fact, long before we owned it, the farm had help with managing the wildlife (especially what was found in the ponds) from ecology experts, many who were current or former professors from North Carolina State.

One of the experts who helped manage the ponds and wild-life on the Home Place also managed properties for several wealthy businessmen. More than a year after we purchased the farm, he shared with me that a few of those wealthy men were also interested in purchasing the Home Place at the very same time I did.

He called up one of the gentlemen and described the prop-erty, with its white farmhouse and picket fence and beautiful ponds. He reminded the would-be owner of its barns and silos and acres and acres of beautiful earth. He likely talked about how good the land was, how rich in wildlife it was. He knew the Home Place might be the best farm in the region, and the would-be owner knew the property well.

"I think they want six million for it," the manager said. "If you wanted the place, I'd open with an offer of around four million, but I wouldn't pay a penny over four and a half."

"You think they'd sell it for that?" the rich would-be owner said.

"I do," said the manager.

"Well, call them up right now!"

Now, this new bidder had far deeper pockets than Tay and I did. His starting bid was more—*way* more—than what we could afford. Most property owners would salivate over the prospect of a bidding war, particularly when you're talking about high-dollar pieces of real estate that typically take longer to sell. So, when the wildlife manager called up the Home Place owner to make an offer, the owner was just a few words away from what might've been a real estate jackpot.

"Hey, I heard you might be willing to sell your farm," the manager said. "I have someone who might be—"

The owner responded in a way that I can only attribute to divine intervention.

"We're already negotiating with someone," the owner said. "We don't need your help."

Click.

"He hung up the phone on you?" I asked.

"Yeah," the manager replied. "He hung up on me."

I raised my hands to heaven in amazement. "Praise God he did!"

Why would he do that? The farm's owner didn't owe us anything. He didn't feel any particular loyalty to me. To him, I was just a dumb jock with money to spend. But somehow God made it happen. It's as though He hardened the owner's heart to other offers, just like He hardened the heart of Pharaoh when Moses begged him to let his people go (see Exodus 8).

A few weeks later, we closed on the property. The Home Place became First Fruits Farm. The farm I prayed for, the home I dreamed of, was ours.

A Mighty, Miraculous God

Jason Brown, where is your faith? That's how Tay challenged me. Every day since, the challenge has been put before me. *Where is your faith, Jason Brown? Who do you trust? What do you believe?*

Sometimes in this logical, rational, cynical world of ours, we sell God short. We say we have faith. We say we believe in a God of miracles. We read the stories of how, through His power, the Red Sea was parted and the sun stood still. We teach those stories to our children. We tell them how awesome, how powerful, our God is. How He can do anything. Absolutely anything.

But do we believe it? Where is our faith? Do we believe that some challenges are too big for God? That some requests are just too great?

I'm not saying that God will give you every luxury, every earthly delight you ask for. This is not some pitch to embrace a prosperity gospel. I never believed in that. Even if I had, my years on this farm—this miraculous gift from God—would've beaten that belief out of me. We serve God, not the other way around.

But I do believe in a God who can move heaven and earth to fulfill His designs. He can heal relationships that seem impossible to heal. He can orchestrate miracles. He moved a billionaire out of the way so that we could have this farm, and I believe that He can move any mountain, any obstacle, He sees fit to move.

Set foot on First Fruits Farm and you set foot on a miracle. Every rock, tree, and ripple of water, every squirrel and fish and bird, is a testament to God's holy power. Every square inch of the planet contains countless little miracles, of course, but here it's a miracle twice given. The nature around us is a declaration of God's design. The fact that my family is able to enjoy that miracle—to walk through the fields, to gather chicken eggs, to pick fruit, to fish in the lake—is a witness to God's generosity. We're God's children. And like any good father, our heavenly Father wants the best for us. He wants to shower us with love and blessings that fit in His greater purpose.

Where is my faith? Sometimes even today, after I've seen God work so powerfully and so personally in our lives, I'm tempted to place my faith in the wrong things. The temptations and worries of this world push us that way, and sometimes even the most faithful of God's servants can lose sight of where our hope really lies. Then I look out the window and see the provisions of God: the trees, the fields, the pond, the silos. It's a view made possible only, solely, by God's grace.

When I was still in the NFL trying to really follow God—when I handed over my life to Him—He kept bringing me back to the story of Joseph. He was a dreamer and an inter-preter of dreams. And always, without fail, those dreams came true for him. God had a plan for him, just like He has a plan for you and me. The plan wasn't always easy to follow or easy to see, but Joseph trusted.

When I was a child, I dreamed. And my dream came true for me too.

CHAPTER 7

Disaster and Deluge

We had our calling. We had our family—intact and loving, with a new member on the way. We had our farm—the most beautiful farm in North Carolina.

Now we had to do something with it.

It wasn't as if working with the land was completely foreign to me. From Grandpa Jasper and before, I come from a family of farmers. And I got a bit of a green thumb from my father too.

When Ducie and I helped my dad with his landscaping business during the summer, we learned how important the land was and how beautiful it could be with a little work. It seemed like Dad knew how to grow anything. Maybe his biggest skill was in unveiling the finished product. He'd start a job in the morning, ideally after the homeowners had all gone to work. The three of us would work like crazy—planting trees and bushes, grooming flower beds, cutting the grass. Then, late in the afternoon or early evening, the homeowners would come back, see how beautiful their yard looked, and, very often, start tearing up. It was like one of those HGTV big-reveal moments before HGTV was a thing.

Those summers taught me that landscaping was about more than just cutting grass or planting a few flowers. When done right, it could move people deeply, even to tears. For us, the work—at least a lot of the work—was routine. It got to the point where Ducie and I could almost do it blindfolded. But for the people we worked for, the results were never routine. For them, a more beautiful yard was a *blessing*—something that made their lives a little bit better, a little bit more beautiful. Those tiny plots of land became retreats for them—places to unwind after work, sip a lemonade, and get away from the day's stresses. Our labors, in some small way, improved their lives.

Those summers taught me what an awesome impact you can have through service. Working with my dad also familiarized me with some tools and techniques that would come in handy. It taught me how to make vegetation look beautiful. I knew how to plant on a small scale.

But farming? That's completely different. To compare running a farm with landscaping someone's backyard is a little like comparing playing a *real* game of NFL football with firing up *Madden NFL* on your PlayStation. Sure, you can find some similarities, but they go only so far.

When you're dealing with a relatively small suburban yard, you can control that environment to a degree. You calculate most of the variables and inputs. You can test the soil and know that it'll be fairly uniform. You can see how the sun strikes the land and know what'll grow well where. The parameters for the project are cozily limited.

But with a farm, you're dealing with a ton more logistics and challenges. Every acre you manage and every new crop you grow adds new levels of difficulty. You can control some of those variables. You take soil samples all across your farm every two or three years, adding nutrients and adjusting the pH (acidity) levels so that there's a certain amount of consistency and so the soil fits what you want to grow there. You're thinking about runoff and erosion—elements you don't typically have to consider when you've got a small vegetable garden in your backyard. You want whatever topsoil you have to stay good and healthy and in one place for years to come.

And then on the back end, come the harvest, you have to think about how you're going to gather all that food you've actually grown. You've got to have a place to put it or ship it, and you've got to get it there quickly, because fresh produce has a short shelf life. Fruits and vegetables deteriorate, and some deteriorate faster than others. Much of our summer produce—cucumbers and tomatoes and peppers, for instance—must either be chilled right away or go someplace the very day we harvest it. The logistics can be a nightmare at times. First Fruits Farm's main mission is to get food to the people who need it most. Anytime even a little of the food we harvest spoils or goes to waste, we know that we've failed to help someone. A family needed a meal, and we didn't provide it. Farmers must have more than green thumbs. They need to be accountants and scientists and managers and, above all, jugglers—wearing all those hats and handling a ton of details sometimes simultaneously.

But I didn't know hardly any of this when I quit the NFL. Working part time for my dad's landscaping business didn't prepare me for it all. I wasn't necessarily starting off at ground zero, but my expertise in *this* field of play was pretty narrow.

So I started watching YouTube videos.

Online Agriculture Education

People laugh at me when I tell them that. "Really?" they say. "You learned how to farm through YouTube?" But, for me, it was very natural—thanks to football.

When you play for the NFL, a big part of your job is watching film. We studied hours and hours of game film every single day. You break down your own work from the last game, using it to correct your mistakes and improve. You study film of your opponent, looking for the tiniest tendencies and tells that might help give you an advantage. Some days you can watch so much video that you walk away bleary eyed. But all those hours in the film room taught me how to break down what I saw on video and emulate it.

So, when I started watching YouTube videos on how to farm, I felt right at home. It was natural for me to learn that way—watching those experienced farmers plow and plant and tend to their crops. I'd watch the videos, break them down, and have full confidence that I could reproduce what I saw on my own farm.

That wasn't the only area where my first career helped me pursue my second. Football and farming share more similarities than you'd think. First, they both take place on a field, though the ones I "play" on these days aren't marked off by the yard. Both require a great deal of planning and preparation, and both can be incredibly physically demanding. Both even have a sort of playbook, though for farmers, our playbook is the *Farmers' Almanac*. It's filled with tons of information you need in farming, from long-term weather trends to gardening tips to recipes for how to cook what you just grew. The similarities between football and farming are endless. So even though I was stepping into unfamiliar waters, I found that many things felt surprisingly similar. Although I couldn't anticipate every challenge that farming would entail, the familiarity I felt with some aspects of my new career helped me take the inevitable challenges in stride.

In fact, when the first storm of my new career blew in, it didn't hit the farm at all. It hit the bank.

Cash and Crops

We bought First Fruits Farm in late 2012. I wasn't planning on starting to farm until 2014. We wanted to concentrate on getting our hundred-year-old farmhouse renovated and brought up to code—a suitable place to raise what we hoped would be a large family. We needed to make plans for how this farming business would work. Farming is expensive. You've got to have the right equipment, and that costs money. You've got to budget for fuel and maintenance. Hiring the labor to get it all done can be pricey as well. We never planned on donating *everything* we grew to charity. I didn't know exactly how the harvest ratios would break down yet—how much we'd donate and how much we'd sell. But I envisioned that we'd probably give away 10 to 20 percent of our crop and then market and sell the rest to cover the farm's overhead.

Tay and I weren't necessarily expecting to turn a profit from First Fruits Farm, not with the charity work we wanted to do as part of it. Our goal was simply to break even. But breaking even would've been just fine, because the NFL had made me a pretty wealthy man. And I was expecting to stay that way.

That would've made me an exception to the NFL rule.

Listen, not many NFL players are hurting for cash while they're competing. In fact, most professional athletes—at least the athletes in major televised sports—make a pretty good living as long as they're active. If you play in the NFL for a handful of years, and as long as you're not crazy stupid with your money, you're going to leave the sport reasonably wealthy.

Sadly, few NFL players stay that way. Some years ago, *Sports Illustrated* found that 78 percent of NFL players either declare bankruptcy or are in dire financial straits just two years after they leave the league. For every Josh Jacobs, who grew up homeless before finding fame and fortune in the league, you have players who find themselves following the opposite trajectory: they find unimaginable wealth while playing and then become destitute later. For many, professional sports can be a rags-to-riches-to-rags story.

Why do athletes tend to fall on such hard times? Sometimes these players' lives are upended by problems that followed them to the NFL or that the NFL's lavish lifestyle encourages. Drug addiction can be an all-too-common problem for many. But often it's just financial mismanagement. Not many folks have experience handling seven- or eight-figure salaries, and often players don't know how to handle all that money that comes pouring in. They spend it almost as soon as they make it, imagining that it'll never run out. Many give extravagant gifts and loans to friends or family members who, of course, never pay them back. And sometimes they simply make bad investment decisions.

When I left the league, I was determined that wasn't going to be me. I'd funneled money into what seemed like smart investments. And just like the experts say, I diversified. If one investment avenue blew up, the others would still be making money. I invested close to $5 million in stocks with a massive, well-regarded national institution. The company knew a thing or two about investments.

I had another $3 million invested in a promising indoor aquaculture business—a fishery, in other words. The aquaculture industry was booming in Maryland at the time, and

Waterland Fisheries—the company I invested in—was doing a strong business in farming tilapia. In 2008, when they shipped their first batch of fish, they planned to eventually raise as much as 1.5 million pounds of fish every year.

And then, knowing that the bulk of my money was in some reasonably safe investments, I took another $500,000 and started a venture-capital group with a couple of other investors—a company that took risks in start-up businesses like you see on the show *Shark Tank*.

I assumed this would make for a pretty healthy nest egg. Based on the history of these investments, I was anticipating returns of around $1 million annually. If I hadn't owned the farm—if I'd just settled into retirement—those proceeds would be enough to live off comfortably for a long, long time. It was also enough to get First Fruits up and running. We could buy the equipment we needed with that money. We could purchase seeds and fertilizer. We'd be able to hire help. And in the coming years, if the harvest wasn't strong or the market went south, my NFL income would give my family and me enough to live on. We wouldn't have to worry and stress over weather and pests like most other farmers do. We had a backup—a cushion—to soften whatever blows might come our way.

I didn't think Tay and I would have to worry about finances for the rest of our lives. Whatever God had called us to do on our farm—whatever crazy ideas He might have up His sleeve—I knew I had the resources to see those ideas through. Like Joseph in the Bible, I'd stored up my wealth. Even if my farm struggled, I was ready.

Being comfortable financially allowed me to be comfortable with this new life.

Comfortable. I laugh at that word now.

Those who follow a prosperity-gospel form of Christianity believe that God wants us to be comfortable and that He'll provide us the means to find us that comfort. They think, *Oh, I'm going to follow Jesus all the way to a comfortable life.* But that's not what Jesus says at all. He tells us, "Look, if you're going to be My disciple, you're going to have to measure the cost" (see Luke 14:27–33). Even Jesus—the very Son of God—wasn't comfortable in His time on earth: "Foxes have holes, and birds of the air have nests, but the Son of Man has nowhere to lay his head," He says in 9:58. Jesus is telling us, "Hey, I don't even have a bed to sleep in at night. I'm about My Father's business." He didn't care about comfort. He wasn't looking for comfort. He had a job to do.

I knew all that. I was very aware that my comfortable life had contributed to an impoverished relationship with God—that money can sometimes be a spiritual distraction. But now my money was invested for *ministry.* Instead of working for me, my finances were going to work for God and for the security and stability of us, his dutiful servants. God would honor that devotion, right?

God had already been incredibly generous to me and my family. He restored and redeemed us, setting us on a better, more loving path. He'd given us a farm. We saw yet more evidence of that in December 2012, when we welcomed our third child. Noah was born at the farm, not at the hospital—yet another gift. I knew God's generosity would continue. *God is good, all the time.* That's what the song says, and the Brown family was living proof of it.

But I wanted to take the next step—to go deeper in my relationship with God. So, in that period of calm and comfort, I prayed a new prayer.

"God, You're amazing," I said. "You've done some amazing things in my life. You've just begun writing a beautiful testimony in my life—a *real* testimony that will make people think about You and Your goodness. I know that there's so much more to write, God. Keep developing my testimony. Make my life something that when people look at me, when people hear my story, they can't help but see You through it all."

Then I said something I hadn't planned on praying. To this day, I don't know why I prayed it. Maybe I knew that for people to see God in my life, they'd need to see, to *feel*, how much I trusted Him to take care of me, in good times and bad. I wanted to emulate the heroes in the Bible—those people who were so close to the Almighty that they relied on Him as they would a flesh-and-blood father.

I added, "God, I want You to take me to a place where I depend on You. Where I lean on You for everything. Where I cry out to You, God."

Be careful what you pray for.

Flood

As we were renovating the farmhouse and caring for our new baby, Noah, we began to experience a storm of our own. Stocks were hot in 2013. The Dow-Jones Industrial Average rose 26 percent that year. The S&P 500 did even better.

Everyone was making money. Except for me.

We trusted our financial adviser at that large investment firm. We had faith that she would make wise decisions that would not just preserve the principal we gave her but also earn a healthy return. That didn't happen. Our adviser dropped the ball countless times. Every month, our balance dropped. Every month, our principal diminished until it was almost entirely gone, drowned in a deluge of bad financial decisions. When I asked her what had happened to the millions we had given her, the millions we had *entrusted* to her, she made no apologies and certainly made no amends.

"Mr. Brown, you know there are no guarantees with the stock market," she said. "You know that when we entered into our financial arrangement, you signed *this* disclosure and *that* disclaimer, right? I'm sorry, Mr. Brown, but there's nothing we can do. Your losses are your losses."

Honestly, I still don't know what happened—if there might be some recourse that we could take, some person or some company that we could blame. Was it the market? Was it the adviser? I don't have the financial savvy or the time to dive into the issue myself. And for the past several years, we haven't had the money to hire an attorney to explore the issue for us.

Meanwhile, Waterland Fisheries was going under too. The fishery, which had become the largest seafood producer in Maryland, had been battered by storms, and in late 2012, the roof literally fell in on the business. When the company turned to its insurance provider for the funds to rebuild, the provider didn't want to honor the insurance claim. Waterland took the insurance company to court, and eventually they settled. Apparently, that settlement didn't save the aquaculture business, which went bankrupt. Not long after, it closed its doors for good, and all its tangible assets were sold off. Those sales didn't help Waterland's investors (like me) recoup any money. When the company was liquidated, the banks were the first in line to use its assets to pay off some outstanding loans. I received nothing.

For years, I'd put a good chunk of my NFL paychecks into these investments—investments that I knew I'd need to rely on when my playing days were done. Now almost all that money was gone, as if a malicious magician had pointed his magic wand at it and caused it to disappear. The most frustrating thing was that I felt utterly helpless. I'd made my fortune based on passion and determination and hours and hours of work, but none of this was going to get my money back. It felt like the whole series of events was completely out of my control. There was nothing I could do. It was as if I were drowning.

As I watched most of our family's money wash away, I told Tay about our financial reversals. There wasn't much I could say beyond that.

"I don't know what's going on, dear," I said. "I don't have any answers."

When we got married, she promised to be with me for better or worse, for richer or poorer. Well, I had to tell her that we were definitely now poorer.

We still had one last financial resource left: the cash I had invested with this venture-capital group. But when I went to investigate reclaiming that emergency fund, I found out that even *that* money was gone, possibly through embezzlement. Despite our inquiries and an investigation into that partner, we have no clear answers about what happened to our money.

The only thing I knew—knew for sure—was that most of the money I had counted on to start a new life was gone.

As I said, so many former NFL players get into financial trouble after they retire, and I planned to be an exception. I wasn't. In 2012, I'd been a wealthy man, financially ready and able to dive into a new life and prepared for all its risks and expenses. A year later, most of my worldly resources had been washed away and we didn't have an income. Yes, we had our farm, and my money wasn't *completely* wiped away. We still had enough in the bank to pay our basic bills and put food on the table. God had blessed us with our daily bread. But the cash we needed to begin to farm in earnest? That simply wasn't there. We had no money for equipment, no money for labor. We didn't even have the funds to buy seed. For the first time since college, we were struggling. It was as if I'd never played in the NFL, never signed those contracts.

I'd been a good servant, hadn't I? We lived on the most beautiful farm in North Carolina—a place that God had miraculously provided for us. We were doing our best to follow His new plan for our lives. We were serving Him. We were doing His bidding.

What happened?

No miracles came to fill our bank account with funds that year. As much as I might've hoped that this whole series of disasters was nothing more than a bad dream, I wasn't waking up. I felt confused, lost, hurt, adrift. I felt like Job, who helplessly watched his family and fortune vanish until he was all alone, left to scrape his boils with a piece of broken pottery. I felt alone too. Abandoned. Honestly, I felt forsaken by God.

All those emotions—the confusion, the hurt, the sadness— eventually coalesced into a new emotion: anger.

I wasn't angry with God. Not at first. I felt it was *Satan's* doing. "The thief cometh not, but for to steal, and to kill, and to destroy," Jesus tells us in John 10:10 (KJV). "I am come that they might have life, and that they might have it more abundantly."

Satan came and *stole* from me. As he did so, he tried to kill and destroy my dreams. But you know what? With every week that brought more bad news, with every day that sapped more of our resources, I grew angrier with God, too, because He allowed it all to happen. Where was the abundance that Jesus promised me in John 10:10? Why was God allowing the abundant resources that I already *had*—abundance that I was using for *His* purposes—to all be taken from me?

One night, I poured out all my hurt and anger in prayer. I wanted God to reverse it all.

"God, I'm working for You!" I told Him. "How can You allow these resources to be taken away from me? I need them— not for me, but for You! I need to have the money to do what You want me to do! You need to go to Satan and redeem and restore everything that was *stolen* from me!" I said. "Make me *whole* again!"

Then God put me in my place.

Jason, don't be so quick to point the finger, He told me. *You're giving the devil too much credit. Remember all those years when you didn't pray to Me? When you didn't show your need for Me? When you didn't place your faith in Me? When all your faith was in your bank account?*

You asked for this, Jason. You asked Me to write your testimony. You asked Me to take you to a place of humility. Didn't you say to Me, "Take me to a place where I depend on You. Where I lean on You for everything. Where I cry out to You, God"?

Cry out to Me now, Jason, God said. *Cry out to Me now.*

So I did. I fell to my knees and cried—cried to heaven.

The Corruption of Comfort

"Naked came I out of my mother's womb, and naked shall I return thither," Job says. "The LORD gave, and the LORD hath taken away; blessed be the name of the LORD" (Job 1:21, KJV).

I think about that last sentence—how the Lord giveth and the Lord taketh away.

We know that God wants to shower us with blessings. We know from the Bible that nothing evil can come from Him. So, when we have reversals and suffer setbacks, when we go through life's trials and tribulations, we ask why. It's only human to ask why. We associate those trials with evil. And so naturally, if we're Christian and we're suffering through difficult times, we point to the Adversary—to Satan. It's *his* fault, we say.

But at the same time, Job learned that God allows these things to happen.

When we pray for patience, God rarely just taps us on the shoulder and gives it to us. He takes us through a time when we're forced to learn that patience. When we pray for humility, He leads us to a place where we are humbled. When we ask to have a deeper relationship with Him, sometimes He pushes us to a place where we have to talk with Him every day, every hour.

And sometimes when we question God about our trials and moments of suffering, He roars into our lives and talks to us, like He did with Job.

> Who is this that darkens counsel by words
>   without knowledge?
> Dress for action like a man;
> I will question you, and you make it known
>   to me. (38:2–3)

God eventually restored Job's fortune. But He hasn't restored mine. He didn't magically return my wealth. For the next several years, and to this day, Tay and I have struggled financially. We budget as tightly as if we were still in college. My wife has worked part time here and there to pay the bills, and sometimes we've paid them late. Most people think I'm still a millionaire, but there've been times when I didn't have a hundred dollars in the bank.

It hasn't been easy these past several years. If money was a temptation when I played football, the lack of money opened the doors to different temptations. This beautiful farm sometimes has felt like an anchor around my neck. Like the Hebrews who escaped from Egypt and retroactively thought of their captivity as the good old days, I've sometimes looked back at my life before First Fruits and remembered those times when I didn't worry about the utility bill, or when I could just go out and buy a new vehicle if I needed one.

When those financial reversals first hit, it was so tempting to walk away from farming. It would've been so easy.

When all these money problems first happened, I could've called Harold, my agent, again. "I know I've been out for a year or two, but could you try to schedule workouts with a few teams?" I could've asked. A team would've taken a chance on me, and I would've made good on their faith. I had something left in the tank, another few good NFL years left in me. Another year or two of football, and we'd be back on solid ground.

Or I could've turned to Tay and asked her to be the primary breadwinner in the home. As I said, she works a couple of days a week now, but what if she went to work full time? She has a doctorate. She could easily make well over six figures.

Or we could sell the farm. And make no mistake, I *have* been tempted. First Fruits is a desirable property in a desirable location. We could put the place up for sale, and one of those millionaires or billionaires would snap it up for, *easily,* twice what we paid for it.

When you're drowning, you start thrashing and flailing around, hoping to find anything that floats. You panic. You look for something to save you. Sometimes, selling First Fruits Farm looks like a tempting life preserver. It's so tempting, when your faith is wavering a little, to do what I had so often before becoming a farmer: forget my reliance on God and instead rely on my own resources to save me. We could sell the farm, take the money, and live comfortably for the rest of our lives.

Comfort. There's that word again.

But following God isn't comfortable.

Ask Job. Ask Joseph. Ask almost anyone who sincerely decides to pursue God's call. I didn't call myself to do this; *God* called me. The evidence is all around me, and new proof pops up every year. He might not have restored my fortune, but He did restore my family—a gift far more valuable than a fat bank account. God has blessed us immensely—not always in ways that show up on a spreadsheet, but in ways that I can feel around the dinner table, when I lead family devotions, and when I wake up in the morning and watch the sun rise over my farm.

So, for me to turn my back on God's call, to sell the farm— that'd be like saying that *God* made a mistake. I know for a fact that He didn't do so. God doesn't make mistakes.

I think about how we saw His hand in giving us the very farm we'd be selling—how he shoved a millionaire or billionaire out of the way. I think about all the miracles we've seen since. The fact that First Fruits exists at all is no accident. Its birth, just like my own and your own, was designed and planned and orchestrated by God. It's not my farm; it's His. I'm only His caretaker. His steward. I've seen His hand powerfully at work in this place. How could I hand it to someone else?

And here's the thing: as poor as we might've felt, we were in a position to see how much real poverty there was, even in North Carolina. Families are going without medicine and shelter, and far too many families are going hungry.

When we bought First Fruits Farm, we gave it that name for a reason. The first fruits would go to charities and food banks around the region. But after our first harvest—when we gave away every sweet potato we grew—the people who ran these charities came back and asked, "Do you have any more? Our food banks are depleted." The cupboards, for so many of these organizations, were bare.

So God placed in our hearts the desire to keep giving. In faith. Every year. Even in our relative poverty, even when it seemed as though we couldn't afford it, we've given our harvest away.

Two Lottery Tickets

Our finances were in shambles for years after that. And because we were giving our harvests away, our bank accounts weren't getting any fatter.

A few years ago, one of the national lottery jackpots—I think it was for Mega Millions—was getting close to a billion dollars. A billion dollars! As I was pumping some gas, I saw the sign displaying how much the jackpot was worth.

Wow, we could really use a few hundred million dollars, I thought, considering my own empty checking account. On impulse, I walked into the gas station and bought a couple of tickets.

But as I drove home with those tickets in my pocket, I started crying. I was literally sobbing in the driver's seat.

"I'm so sorry, God!" I wailed as I drove. "God, what did I do?"

See, when you walk by faith, it's not a lottery mentality. We're supposed to look to God for our daily bread. And for years, that's what we'd been doing. No matter how tight our finances were, no matter that there were months we didn't know how we were going to pay the utility bill, we walked in faith. We looked and prayed to God for our daily bread. We didn't trust in some lottery ticket—that somehow a bunch of money would fall from the sky and we'd be wealthy all of a sudden. It doesn't work that way.

I drove into the farm and walked into the house. Tay immediately saw that my eyes were all red. Tears were still on my cheeks.

"Jason, what's wrong?" she asked.

"Dear, I just bought a couple of lottery tickets."

She gasped in horror. "Oh no! Why did you do that?"

The tears started again. "I don't know why, dear!" I blubbered.

We both felt terrible and turned to God in prayer. "God, please, *please,* don't let us win."

Who does that? I know that many Christians buy lottery tickets all the time, maybe every week, and think nothing of it. To many people—even people who don't buy lottery tickets—this whole story feels a little silly. Why all the remorse? Why all the repentance for just a couple of little lottery tickets?

But it's what happened. And it's because we remembered. We remembered what it was like to have money. To have all the luxuries that money can buy. Yet with all that money, our hearts weren't in the right place. We were focused on the material things of the world, not the eternal things of God.

People often misquote the Scriptures, saying that money is the root of all evil. That's not really what it says. It says the *love* of money is the problem (see 1 Timothy 6:10). It's too easy to be focused on material things, to be just so overwhelmed when your life and so many of your priorities are dominated by money. It becomes more than a distraction; it becomes a burden.

Buying those lottery tickets wasn't evidence that we loved money, but it was a sign that we still wanted to rely on it. *Remember when you didn't place your faith in Me?* God asked me. *When all your faith was in your bank account?* I did remember. I didn't want to go back to that time. And so we cried. We repented. "God, please forgive us," Tay and I said. "All we need is You. We don't need all that other stuff anymore."

#blessed

People talk about blessings all the time. Look at social media and you'll see plenty of folks talk about how #blessed they are. They'll post pictures of their new BMWs and write, "#blessed." They'll tweet from a beach in Maui and add, "#blessed."

As if God exists only to shower them with material goods.

But the blessings extend far beyond big houses and fancy cars and *comfort*. I had all that stuff, but those weren't blessings. The real blessings of God aren't things we can wear or drive or put in a bank account; rather, we are truly blessed when we feel God's presence in our lives. After all, God's greatest blessing is *Himself.* He gave Himself to us for our sins. He blessed us with new life. And if we pay attention, we see that He blesses us with His presence all the time.

I could've gone back to the NFL, but I would've missed so many blessings. My marriage is strong. I feel closer to God now than I ever did when I was living in an MTV-style crib. I have seen God at work in this farm. I have seen Him at work in me and my family, bringing us so far in our love for Him and each other in so short a time.

Tay could've gone back to work full time, but then we wouldn't be able to homeschool our children. We would've turned them over to strangers every weekday and allowed those strangers to teach them and raise them and instill them with their *own* values, not ours. Now we're able to train them up in the ways of the Lord (see Proverbs 22:6)—to teach them what we value and who we worship in a way that we'd never be able to otherwise.

We could've sold the farm. But how many blessings would we have missed then? How many miracles would we have never seen? How many chances to see God in action would we have lost?

After retiring from the NFL, I thought I'd never be hurting for money again. I was wrong. But when my worldly blessings were gone, it opened the floodgates for miracles. And some were just around the corner.

CHAPTER 8

Sweet, Sweet Potatoes

Broke. Exhausted. Abandoned. That's where I found myself
that hot summer day in 2014—the day you've already caught a
glimpse of. My NFL career was gone. All the money I'd made
playing football was gone. *Maybe God* did *give us this farm*, I
thought. But we had nothing else. No labor. No equipment.
No seed money.

"God!" I shouted.

I didn't see any miracles on the horizon at the time. All I saw
was the dust. The stubborn ground. The clouds of mosquitoes.

The tractor, that 1968 Allis-Chalmers, groaned and sput-
tered.

"God! I don't mind praying to You, but every time I get on
this thing, do I have to pray that it starts up?"

It all felt like a cruel joke. We left a life of comfort to follow
God to what we thought would be our own Promised Land. I
had told my son that this was a land of milk and honey, filled

with riches and gifts beyond measure. But now it felt like a wilderness, a thousand acres that I was cursed to wander across. People already thought I was insane. They'd be laughing at me now, mocking this crazy Christian and his dream of being a farmer for God. As for God Himself . . . well, I knew He was with us still. In my heart, deep down, I knew He wouldn't desert us. But in that moment, in the heat and the mosquitoes, I sure didn't see Him. I didn't feel Him. I felt forsaken. It was as if God had driven us to a strange new life, kicked us out of the car, and taken off.

We had a farm, but would we ever plant anything on it? Seemed unlikely. To grow a crop, you needed seeds. To grow a crop, you needed a real tractor. I'd suffered setbacks and trusted God. I felt the laughter and trusted Him. But now, as the Allis-Chalmers grumbled, I'd had enough.

"God!" I shouted a third time into the blue sky, empty land surrounding me for at least a square mile. "I don't even have to do this, all right? I'm out here for *You*! I'm doing this for *You*! I'm working faithfully for *You*!"

I looked around the empty field and thought about the farmers nearby.

"All these other farmers," I said. "Look at them with their nice new John Deere tractors. *They* don't work for You, but *I* do!"

I grew bold.

"You know what, God? I'm going to *need* me one of them daggone tractors! And You know what? You're gonna get me one of them daggone tractors! I don't know how You're going to do it, but You're going to do it!"

Call it a prayer. Call it a tantrum. Call it whatever you want. But I was hurting. I was tired. And I was calling out to my heavenly Father—telling my Daddy what I needed. And I wasn't done.

"God, by this time next year, You're going to *bless* me with one of those tractors," I said. "It's going to need at least a"—I thought for a moment—"a *hundred* horsepower, because this is a *big* farm! And it's going to need some sort of four-wheel drive because of all the hills around here! And—"

I slapped at a horsefly on my neck.

"And, God? I'm tired of swatting all these flies out here and getting all hot and sweaty in the summertime! That tractor needs to be *enclosed* and *air-conditioned,* all right?"

It was just me and God out there. Me and God and all the mosquitoes and flies. God asked me to cry out to Him. Well, that's what I did that afternoon: I cried out to Him, cried out like a baby. And finally, after my energy had been spent and my tears had dried, I stopped.

"Amen," I said. And I went back to work.

Whatever God had in store for me, I knew it wasn't going to come that afternoon. I still had work to do. I didn't have any money, but I wasn't going to let that stop me from being a farmer. I had a field to get ready for sweet potatoes.

From YouTube to My Tubers

Sweet potatoes and North Carolina have had a long, productive relationship. Native Americans grew the vegetable here well before it was called North Carolina, and now the state grows more sweet potatoes than anywhere else in the country. The potatoes love the rich soil and warm weather, and they can't stand frost, which makes the state perfect for them. North Carolina farmers dedicate more than ninety-five-thousand acres of land to the crop annually, and they supply 60 percent of the country's sweet-potato needs. The sweet potatoes are really healthful, filled with vitamins and minerals and antioxidants. Some scientists say that eating them can help ward off certain types of cancer. And because they're grown from transplants, or "slips," instead of seeds, they're relatively easy to grow.

All of that made it an ideal first crop for First Fruits Farm. *If* I had any money. *If* I knew what I was doing. But I was determined to walk in faith. And everyone knows that any walk—in faith, in farming, in anything else—requires a first step.

I called up my neighbor Len Wester, owner of one of the biggest farming operations in the area. He and his family have been working the land for nearly a hundred years now, and every year he farms several thousand acres, making it one of the region's largest farms. He understands the North Carolina soil, and how to work it, better than anyone I know. He also had heard much of my story—how this stupid ex–football player wanted to be a farmer and grow food for the poor. If anyone could help me figure out those first steps toward a successful sweet-potato crop, it'd be Len.

"Hey, Len, I need some help," I said over the phone. "I'd like to grow five acres of sweet potatoes. You know that hill on the backside of my farm? I'd like to plant them in the field there. But—well, I don't know anything about sweet potatoes."

"Well, you know what, Jason?" Len said. "I don't know anything about sweet potatoes either."

Before I had a chance to be too disappointed, Len added, "But I have some buddies out east, and they grow thousands of acres of sweet potatoes. That's what they do. Let me ask them if they'd be willing to help."

Those buddies were David and Allen Rose, who run another huge farming operation near Nashville, North Carolina. The farm, J. B. Rose and Son, sprawls over thousands of acres, and the brothers typically grow not just sweet potatoes but cotton and soybeans and cucumbers as well.

I didn't tell Len about my financial problems. I still didn't know how I was going to be able to afford to plant anything. But remember, God told me to walk in faith. This was the next step in that walk: learning how to actually plant and grow what I wanted. And in the meantime, I prayed—prayed that God would open some unexpected door, some window, some *keyhole*. That God would somehow facilitate what He had called me to do.

About a month after that initial call, Len called me back.

"Hey, Jason, let's go look at that field of yours," he said. "The field up on the hill where you wanted to plant those sweet potatoes."

So I went. And there I saw a miracle.

The field, from one side to the other, all five acres, had already been dug, prepped, and rowed. The ground was covered in ripples of earth: rows of raised hills about six or eight inches high, running all the way to the trees beyond, separated by furrows where the water collects and irrigates the crops.

All along the tops of those rows—those ripples of land undulating over the field—I saw small sprouts of green. The sweet-potato slips were already in the ground.

I was shocked. I had asked for *advice,* not a fully planted field full of sweet potatoes. I didn't know what to say. I didn't even know what it *meant*. I was grateful, but I was worried too. Had I miscommunicated with Len? Did he think that I had asked him to *plant* this field for me and I was now on the hook for what it cost?

"Man, what's going on?" I said when I found my voice.

"Well, me and my guys, we had the afternoon off," Len told me, talking about some of his farmhands. "I just figured we could come over here and knock this out for you."

"Well, that's great, Len," I said cautiously. Len is a super guy, but he's a savvy farmer too. He knows that time is money.

To "knock out" a five-acre field cost him plenty. And on an operation like his, it'd be unusual for him and his employees to have an afternoon to kill. "But how much did all this cost?"

"Well," Len began, "usually, sweet-potato slips run about $1,000 an acre."

I couldn't believe what I was hearing. This was just like what you worry about with a car mechanic, fixing a whole bunch of stuff that you never authorized. I was looking at five acres of planted sweet potatoes. That's $5,000 worth of transplants. I didn't have $5,000 to give him. I didn't even have *$500*. I had put my faith in God that He would somehow give me the means to afford a crop this year—maybe not enough to cover all five acres I'd set aside, but *something*. Something to show that I was serious about farming, that I was serious about following God's call. And now, after all my financial setbacks, after all the stumbling blocks I'd suffered the past few months, here looked like another: a field of sweet potatoes I couldn't pay for.

"Um, Len, I *really* wish you had told me that," I said.

"No, no," Len said with a smile. "Don't worry about it. David and Allen—you know, the Rose brothers I told you about—I talked to them about you. They know what you're trying to do here. They know that you're trying to grow and give food to the needy. Their hearts were so touched by what you're doing that they donated all this.

"Jason, they *gave* you all these transplants."

I couldn't believe it. *Thank You, God,* I prayed silently.

"But what about you, Len?" I said. The Rose brothers might've donated the slips, but Len and his crew did the work. From experience, I knew it couldn't have been easy.

"You know what?" he said. "We'll figure it out later. We'll work it out sometime."

That was more than six years ago. I'm still trying to figure out what "work it out" means. I've never gotten a bill. I've never gotten an invoice. He never mentioned it again.

Len died February 29, 2020, as I was writing this book.

His obituary reminds people what a great man he was in the community, what a loving husband and father and grandfather he was. It says that he loved racing Matchbox cars with his grandkids and that he was an enthusiastic poker player.

The obituary doesn't mention how Len Wester helped a new neighbor when that neighbor needed help the most. It doesn't say that if it hadn't been for Len's kindness and generosity, there might not have been a First Fruits Farm.

A Career That Demands Faith

I don't know how you could be a farmer and not have faith. Everything we do is an act of faith—a statement of belief.

Yes, a lot of that faith is built on knowledge and preparation. Before we ever put the seeds in the ground, we're making sure the soil's just right and amending it as necessary. We look at long-term weather forecasts to try to help us determine what we should plant, when, and how much. We work hard to eliminate unnecessary variables to give our crops the best opportunity to grow and flourish.

Every seed we plant is still almost a little prayer. When we put it in the ground, it's a way of saying, *I believe. I believe that you'll grow. That you'll be fruitful.* We hope that God will take these seeds and help transform them into something beautiful and useful.

We *all* have a bit of that sort of faith that comes with farming. Even atheists have faith in things they can't see but only hope for. We have faith that the sun will come up. We have faith that gravity will keep working. Think about the cycle of the seasons. Even when we're sweating in July or freezing in February, we know that the weather will change someday. We know, even on the coldest day of winter, that spring is bound to come.

Sometimes it doesn't *feel* like that. It can seem as if the winter will never end—that we'll be dealing with the cold indefinitely. Some people even suffer from seasonal depression, despite logically knowing winter won't last forever. But the cold weather and lack of sun throws off their emotional equilibrium. The cold seeps inside them.

We farmers boldly fight that pessimism in faith. We have to. Many of us start planting seeds when it's still winter, when the cold wind blows over the barren fields and there might still be frost on the ground. Every day that we tend to our crops, tend to our livestock, we're doing so in faith—that all our work will lead to a bountiful harvest. We don't have any guarantees of anything, but none of us ever goes out there, plants a crop, and says, "Well, I might get something this year, or I might not," not really knowing or caring what'll happen. You've got to have faith that your hard work will pay off and that God is with you.

Farming, more than any other profession I know of, gives us a front-row seat for what it looks like to walk in faith every day and what the harvest of that faith can be.

Growing and Giving

All that year, I worked in faith. I tended my five acres of sweet potatoes, watching my YouTube videos and asking other farmers, like Len, for advice when I needed to. I weeded and watered my crops. I tended to them and checked on their progress, digging a few out every now and then to see how they were growing. My borrowed tractor kept chugging away. Everything was working just as it should—just as I thought it would. Unlike with my finances, I did have some control over what was growing on my farm. Thanks to Len and the Rose brothers, and due to some hard work on my part, we were actually going to have a sweet-potato crop this year. And for this first year, we were planning to give it all away.

As I started doing some research, I dug up a new problem. I discovered that one acre of sweet potatoes can yield about twenty thousand pounds. Our five-acre field? If we had a good harvest, that's one hundred thousand pounds. That's a lot of food going to charity—food enough to feed thousands. Praise God, right? But as the potatoes kept growing and the harvest drew closer, I looked around to see what sort of labor we had to harvest all that produce. There was me, of course, and my wife, and . . . well, that was about it. JW was nearly seven by then, but I didn't think we could count on him for much hard labor. Three-year-old Naomi could *carry* a sweet potato or two. *Maybe.* And we weren't about to ask Noah, who was less than two years old, to work the fields for us.

The staff of our farm consisted of just me and my family. That's it. Sure, I knew many people. I still had contact with some of my old football buddies. But they were in the middle of the season. I didn't want to ask anybody to give up all their free time to come down to the farm—to work and sweat and get dirty, just to give all the literal fruits of their labor away. I didn't know what I was going to do.

So, again, I turned to God.

"God, thanks for the blessings You've given us. But like Jesus said in the Bible, 'The harvest is plentiful, but the laborers are few.' "

Don't worry about it, Jason. Don't worry.

"But, God—"

It's just like Field of Dreams. *You plant it, and they will come. I'm going to make sure you have all the help you need. Walk in faith.*

"All right, God," I said. "I don't know what or who's going to come, but I'll leave it in Your hands." So I kept working.

Two weeks later, I received a call from Rebecca Page, the Triangle gleaning coordinator for the Society of St. Andrew.

I didn't know anything about the society at the time. I'd never even heard of it. I only knew who it was named after: Andrew was the disciple who, among other things, told Jesus about the little boy with five loaves of bread and two fishes— food that would wind up feeding five thousand people.

Rebecca quickly explained that the society was a network of people who *glean,* a term used regularly in the Bible. In Leviticus, Israelites are told to not pick clean the corners of the field or gather up the wheat and barley grain that falls to the ground (see 19:9) so that the poor would have something to eat too. Ruth was probably the Bible's most famous gleaner. When the Moabite woman and her mother-in-law, Naomi, migrated to Israel completely destitute, Ruth gleaned the fields of a guy named Boaz. They eventually got married.

Rebecca used the story of Naomi and Ruth as an illustration for what she and her network do. She told me that the society's volunteers—the gleaners—would go out to farms after the main crops had been harvested and gather up the leftovers—the unmarketable fruits and vegetables left out in the field—and deliver them to food banks, church pantries, and soup kitchens. And while the society was (and is) a *nationwide* organization (more than twenty-three thousand people volunteered for the society in 2019), *thousands* of those volunteers lived around the Triangle area of North Carolina, within easy driving distance of First Fruits Farm.

"We heard about your farm," she went on. "We heard that you might have some gleaning opportunities there."

Her call came out of nowhere. I didn't ask them for help. I didn't know anything about the organization five minutes before. But it was, without a doubt, an answered prayer—a prayer answered just the way it needed to be. I was astounded. But now it was my turn to astound her.

"God bless you," I told Rebecca. "But here's the thing: We're not going to have any gleaning opportunities at First Fruits Farm. We're going to have *harvesting* opportunities. You're not just to pick up the leftovers. You're going to have the *best*. In fact, you're going to have it *all*."

Rebecca was, indeed, astounded. The volunteers for St. Andrew rarely have an opportunity to truly harvest food. Most of the thirteen million pounds of produce they collect is stuff that no one else would want. To have an opportunity to work in a field ripe for harvest, filled with all the best produce a farm had to offer? It was a rare treat.

More than six hundred volunteers took advantage of that rare treat on harvest day that fall. We needed every single one of them. God had blessed us with a bumper crop. I had expected 100,000 pounds of sweet potatoes, but instead we pulled more than 120,000 pounds out of that little five-acre field. I connected St. Andrew with Len Wester too. Volunteers gleaned Len's fields and gathered up more than 10,000 pounds of cucumbers. The Society of St. Andrew distributed all that food to churches and food banks across the region.

In our very first year, First Fruits Farm—thanks to help from Len, the Rose brothers, and hundreds and hundreds of volunteers—helped feed thousands of hungry families.

You want to talk about faith that can move mountains? That day, I saw a mountain of sweet potatoes moved, all by faith. I knew I couldn't accomplish that on my own. It was Jesus—the love of Jesus, and the earthbound body of Jesus, the people serving as His hands and feet—that made it possible.

That's what walking in faith can do.

Sowing Seeds

We still give away most of the food we grow. People sometimes ask how we can. And, honestly, sometimes I wonder how we can too. But every year, through God's grace, we've been able to do so. We might not *always* be able to, but so far we have.

How? There's a one-word answer: *God*.

Oh, if you look at our finances, you'll see God at work in pragmatic ways. Tay uses her degree, working as a dentist a couple of days a week. That helps pay the bills. I'm frequently paid to speak at schools, churches, conventions, and the like. Although all that earlier financial turmoil wiped out most of our fortune, I still had a little of it left—enough to cover our expenses. And remember, we *farm*. The house is paid for. We grow most of our own food. Even now that we have eight children in the house, we'll never grow hungry. Tay reminds me that even at our lowest moments here on the farm, we've never reached a point of true poverty, a daily reality for way too many American families.

But sometimes God's provision looks a lot like Len Wester's help or the hundreds of faithful volunteers from the Society of St. Andrew who labored in love. They look a lot like miracles.

In the Parable of the Sower (see Matthew 13), Jesus talks about the frustrations and rewards of farming—how seeds can fall on rocky soil or weeds, how they can be eaten by birds or die in topsoil that's too shallow for them. But the seeds that land in good soil, Jesus says, can yield a tremendous amount of fruit—thirty or sixty or even a hundred times more food than was planted.

Farmers count on a good rate of return. Experts say that when it comes to grain, you need to get at least three seeds back for every one you plant. That's the minimum seed ratio to sustain life, because it gives you two grains to eat for every one that you put away to plant for next year. With today's modern farming techniques, the yield can be much greater. Some years, farmers are even blessed with harvests that outstripped their most optimistic expectations.

In 2014, First Fruits Farm's harvest extended well beyond a bumper crop of sweet potatoes. The farm was experiencing a hundredfold yield in blessings in other areas too—gifts beyond measure. The seeds we were planting were producing fruits we couldn't even conceive of.

A lot of that was because my story was getting out there. Writers and reporters had caught wind of this former professional football player who'd become a farmer and how he was giving food away to those who needed it. It was a weird story, a compelling story, a feel-good story that'd make readers and listeners and viewers feel better after sifting through all the *real* news, stories about bitter politics and disaster and scandal. It was the sort of news that would make folks feel a little better about the world around them—that some good was left in it still.

We owed much of that interest to Tim Stevens, a sports reporter for North Carolina's *News & Observer*. He had come out to the farm in 2013 and reported on First Fruits Farm and all my big plans for the place then, and he came out again to follow up, right during our incredible harvest in 2014.

He took some pictures, wrote a nice little piece on the harvest, and guess what? That story went all around the world. Suddenly, First Fruits Farm became a coast-to-coast feel-good story, and national journalists started knocking on our farm door to talk with us. Our email was inundated with well wishes. We were getting thank-you notes in the mail. (We started getting plenty of unsolicited advice too: "Hey, here's what you should *really* be growing on your farm," they'd write.) It was all very gratifying.

As nice as all the publicity was, we didn't get very many donations out of it. Admittedly, we weren't really soliciting any. As far as the world outside our farmhouse walls thought, I was still a rich former NFL player. People assumed I had all the money in the world to do what I was doing. *He doesn't need my help,* many people likely were thinking. That was just fine. I didn't want them to know that I *needed* help either. I was a big, strong ex–football player. I was used to pushing around three-hundred-pound nose tackles. I sure wasn't going to admit weakness. I wasn't going to tell people that my fortune had drained away.

But one man who heard our story *did* come forward with an unusual offer.

"I think it's great what you guys are doing," the gentleman (who prefers to remain anonymous) said in an email shortly after our story went viral. "I was really touched. And I wanted to know: Do you need any equipment? If I can help you, please contact me."

I didn't bother. I went on to other things and nearly forgot the offer.

There's an old joke about a preacher stuck in a flood, sitting on top of his roof. He prays to God, begging for help. A man comes by in a boat and tells him to hop in.

"No," the preacher says. "I'm praying to God."

The waters keep rising. Another man comes by in a speedboat, offering to help. The preacher says no. He rejects help from a rescuer in a helicopter too. He rejects all aid, but the preacher continues to pray to God to save him until, in the end, the floodwaters cover him.

When he gets to heaven, the preacher walks up to God and says, "I'm glad I'm here, God, but why didn't You save me?"

God looks at him and says, "What more did you want from Me? I sent you two boats and a helicopter."

I was like that preacher on the roof. In my pride, I didn't want to accept help from a stranger. I wanted God to bless me, but I wanted Him to bless me the way I thought He *should* bless me. In a way that I expected Him to bless me, not through a stranger's email. We barely had the money to keep the internet on, but I let the gentleman's note go without even a response.

Two weeks later, he wrote back.

"Hey, I love what you guys are doing," it said. "I still want to help if I can. Let me know." There was a phone number in the email too.

This time, Tay wasn't going to let the opportunity go.

"Jason, please humble yourself," she said. "This might be just what you were praying for, all right? Just talk to this gentleman."

I probably sighed heavily. I was thinking there was no way this "gentleman" was all he presented himself to be. He couldn't be interested in only helping us, no matter how touched he said he was by our story. If he'd just sent twenty dollars to us, we would've accepted it gladly. But offering help in buying equipment? There was more to it than that. There had to be.

But I called him up—to make Tay happy.

He answered the phone and seemed glad I called. He repeated how much he valued what we were doing. He repeated his offer to help with equipment. When I didn't answer right away, he went on.

"So, can I help you with anything? Any equipment you need for the farm? Some machinery? An attachment for your tractor?"

Tractor. Months before, I'd been weeping and shouting in my field. The flies had been biting me. My borrowed Allis-Chalmers sounded like it was dying. In my frustration and my anger and my desperation, I'd called out for something.

"Sir, I *have* been praying for something, actually," I finally blurted. "I've been praying for a tractor."

Just like that, the gentleman on the other end of the phone was off and running.

"A tractor!" he said. "Of course! You'd *need* a good tractor with as big a farm as you have. A *really* good tractor, a reliable one. Something like a John Deere," he said. "At least a hundred-horsepower one, I'd imagine."

"It gets pretty hot out there, too, doesn't it?" he added, barreling on. Before I could answer, he said, "Yep, it needs to have an enclosed cab. With air-conditioning."

He started rattling off not just what my tractor needed but what I'd *asked* for, as if he'd been standing beside me in the field that day. He kept talking about *my* tractor, a tractor that no matter *how* good a deal this guy's going to cut for me I know I'll never be able to afford. Finally, I cut him off.

"Hold on a second!" I said. "Listen, I know you're trying to be kind, trying to do me a favor, but I don't know you from Adam. I *do* know that nothing comes for free. What do you want from me? Do you want me to sign autographs? Endorse a product? Do you want me to show up somewhere and make an appearance? A speech? What's the catch? Tell me the catch and *then* maybe we can work on a deal."

I waited for him to speak.

"Jason, God told me to reach out to you and ask if you

needed any help with equipment," he said. "The only obligation you have is to continue being obedient to the Holy Spirit, the same way that I'm being obedient to the Holy Spirit right now."

I didn't know this guy. I didn't know anything about him. He was following a call from God, just like I was. His call was to give me a tractor. Not *work out a great deal* for a tractor—actually *give* me one.

Not long after, he arranged a three-way call with a local John Deere dealer, and the man—I still don't know anything about him—was clearly a fierce negotiator. Some sports agents I know could glean some tips from him. I told the dealer what kind of tractor I needed, and then the gentleman just, well, took over. He talked them down on the price to the point where it was almost ridiculous.

"And another thing," the gentleman told the dealer. "You're going to deliver this tractor to Mr. Brown's farm with a full tank of fuel."

"Um, I'm afraid we don't do that," the dealer said. "We've never delivered a tractor to anyone with a full tank."

"You're going to do it with *this* deal," the gentleman said. If he'd been a coach in the NFL, he could've talked a referee into calling a safety when the line of scrimmage was on the fifty-yard line.

The next day, I got a check in the mail for the tractor, made out to the dealer. A few weeks later, the tractor was delivered to my farm. With a full tank of gas.

That was January of 2015. I'd prayed to God for a tractor the previous summer, asking for a tractor just like the one that, just half a year later, was parked outside my farmhouse.

In my 2014 temper tantrum, I'd asked God to deliver me a great tractor in twelve months. God didn't just answer my prayer; He showed up early.

Overflowing

Walk in faith, God had told me. And so I walked. I walked away from the NFL, walked away from a comfortable life, walked away from all the money I thought I needed to survive in this new adventure. At the beginning of 2014, I didn't have a tractor, didn't have a crop, didn't even have money for seed. I didn't have anything but a hope and a prayer . . . and a God who could do miracles.

A year later, North Carolina's charities had another 120,000 pounds of sweet potatoes to put to use, and I had a tractor that could make sure those potatoes would be an annual gift.

In the book of Joel, we find this passage:

> Be glad, people of Zion,
> > rejoice at what the LORD your God has
> > > done for you.
> > He has given you the right amount of
> > > autumn rain;
> > he has poured down the winter rain for
> > > you
> > and the spring rain as before.
> The threshing places will be full of grain;
> > the pits beside the presses will overflow
> > > with wine and olive oil.
> I will give you back what you lost
> > in the years when swarms of locusts ate
> > > your crops. (2:23–25, GNT)

I know there are people out there—even Christians—who don't believe that God takes an active interest in our lives. I know that some people believe that the age of miracles is long gone. They say that God doesn't part seas for His believers anymore. He doesn't feed five thousand people with a little bit of bread and a couple of fish.

Don't believe that. Our God is a mighty God, and His resources never falter. Using First Fruits Farm, He fed more than five thousand people, using far less than a few loaves and fishes: He used *me*. And He blessed me in the process.

Walk in faith, God told me. And I'd encourage you to do the same. Walk in faith, my brothers and sisters. God has wonderful miracles in store for you.

CHAPTER 9

Failure and
Faithfulness

That first harvest was a game changer. When we bought First
Fruits Farm, many folks around here thought I must've been
crazy—certified insane. No one laughed at me to my face, but
behind my back? Plenty chuckled at this big rich guy without
a clue. And had the situation been reversed—had I been a
longtime North Carolina farmer, and some know-nothing
NFL vet suddenly decided to move next door and grow sweet
potatoes—I might've laughed too. I can't picture Tom Brady
bushwhacking on my land. But sixty tons of potatoes later,
folks weren't laughing at me anymore. I was a success. People
started coming up to me and calling me the sweet-potato whisperer.

I knew that *I* wasn't the reason we had such a successful
harvest. It was all God. I think that He knew that with all the
setbacks I'd suffered, I needed a victory. I'd felt lost. Helpless.
Forsaken. That first year of farming was a morale boost—
confirmation that I was doing the right thing. God was telling

me, *Don't worry, Jason. I haven't left you. I'm here.* God showed up in a big way in 2014, and I couldn't take credit.

Still, sweet-potato whisperer had a nice ring to it!

Yes, I knew God was behind my success. And I assumed that, with God's help, every following year would be just as awesome as the previous one. It's like what Paul wrote in Romans 8:31: "If God is for us, who can be against us?"

And, yes, a little ego started creeping back into my soul. Publicly, I gave God all the credit. Deep inside? I was thinking to myself, *Hey, I'm a pretty good farmer!* Our God is indeed an awesome God, and I was an awesome follower. Together, we'd fill the bellies of the hungry and needy with sweet potatoes.

With my confidence in full swing, and with my pride helping it along, I started running off at the mouth.

"We farmed five acres in 2014? We're going to double it in 2015," I started telling people. "We grew 120,000 pounds of sweet potatoes last year? We're going to harvest *200,000* pounds this year." Truthfully, I thought I was underestimating what First Fruits Farm would produce. I hoped our harvest would be more like 250,000 pounds—another amazing bumper crop. With God in our corner, I figured bumper crops were going to be the norm.

But I wasn't done yet. I planned that after the crop was brought in on November 7, First Fruits Farm would throw an incredible harvest festival for all the volunteers who helped pick sweet potatoes that day. We'd have food. Music. Live entertainment. It was going to be an amazing celebration. We were going to show the world—or, at least, the Triangle area of North Carolina—that our God can do anything.

We planted our fields that spring, and, man, was it beautiful.

And then the rains stopped.

We experienced an extremely dry summer—one of the driest I remember. Without rain, the potatoes struggled to get a footing. And those that did—well, the deer were waiting for them.

While sweet potatoes are a popular crop in North Carolina, I'm the only farmer locally who grows them. Deer, as it turns out, *love* sweet potatoes. They love the vines. They love the potatoes themselves. They love everything about them. They'll dig up the potato plants with their front hooves and pull them straight out of the ground. Although they didn't notice my field in 2014, by 2015, the secret was out. The deer must've spread the news through their secret deer network or talked about it at their local watering hole. They must've said, "Hey, guys, this dumb farmer over here is planting a whole ten-acre crop of sweet potatoes, and it's *just for us!*"

Deer don't have the decency to actually finish eating what they start. They're so trifling that they'll dig up a sweet potato, take one dainty bite of it, and then move on to the next plant. They'll nibble at that second plant for a moment and then, as if unimpressed with the quality of *that* one, too, move down the row to a *third* plant. They're the strangest blend I've ever seen of being completely ravenous and wildly finicky. Do they taste one of my sweet potatoes and say, "Well, that's an okay sweet potato, but the next one's bound to taste so much better"? Are they marking their sweet-potato territory with their teeth?

I'm no deer psychologist, so I can't say. All I know is that after having very little pressure from deer in 2014, an army of the animals seemed to surround every new bit of growth in 2015. If the deer owned an NFL ground mower, they couldn't have cut down my sweet potatoes more efficiently.

The fields looked bleaker and sparser as the summer wore on. We farmers are taught to check on our crops throughout the year—dig up a mound here and there to better estimate what the yield is going to be. And as I dug up my test mounds, the results were . . . not encouraging.

That didn't matter! I still had faith that God would give us a great harvest, just like I'd seen in a movie.

The movie was called *Faith Like Potatoes*, a Christian drama based on a true story. In it, a farmer moves to South Africa, becomes a Christian, and—bucking advice from scientists and fellow farmers and plain old common sense—plants potatoes during a terrible drought. Why? Because the Lord told him to, of course. And his faith was rewarded by a massive harvest of potatoes.

Hey, *I* was a farmer! *I* was called by God! And I grew potatoes too! Sure, my sweet potatoes aren't even that closely related to regular potatoes, but still, I knew that I needed to have *faith like potatoes*. I knew that despite the lack of rain, despite the rather paltry test mounds I was digging up, despite the fact that apparently every deer in North Carolina was migrating to my farm, God was going to do a mighty miracle for us.

"In This World You Will Have Trouble"

We love happy endings. Had this book ended with the 2014 harvest or with my miraculous tractor, it would've been just what Hollywood would want: a happily-ever-after ending, where the crops were always bountiful, the sun always shone, and the deer ate their own dang food.

Look at the Bible and you'll see a more realistic depiction of life. Joseph's deliverance of his brothers led to the captivity in Egypt. Moses's walk out of Egypt got him to the Promised Land, all right, but that land was full of hundreds of years of strife and disobedience. The temple of God was built and torn down, rebuilt and torn down again. Even after we've had great success, life has a frustrating habit of reversing course—sometimes because of our own mistakes, sometimes because God still has lessons to teach us, and sometimes for reasons we might never know until we ask God in person.

"To every thing there is a season, and a time to every purpose under the heaven," Ecclesiastes 3 begins in the King James Version. Football players and farmers, of course, pattern their lives by very literal seasons: With football, you've got the football season (naturally) and the off-season. In farming, you follow spring, summer, and winter religiously—planting early in the year, reaping late.

But those seasons have seasons too—seasons of success and of unexpected challenges.

Sports can teach you how to deal with those highs and lows. When I was with the Ravens, we alternated between winning seasons and losing years like clockwork. Mentally, I knew that farming had its own seasons too. You couldn't grow a bumper crop *every* year. When I had money, I planned to use that cushion to ride out the bad years in preparation for the good ones.

But in 2015, I wasn't ready to accept the ebb and flow just yet. My money was gone, but my faith was full. God loved me; this I knew. And because of that, I figured He wanted to reward my faith with success.

"God, I know You're with me," I said. "There's no failure in You."

As harvest day approached, my sweet potatoes weren't looking any better. Even the deer were losing interest in our scant crop. But I wasn't about to give up. We held a registration for volunteers to help us with our harvest, and more than one thousand people signed up. When we closed down the registration, I kept hearing from more and more people who wanted to come. I didn't want to turn anybody away, so I encouraged anyone who wanted to come pick sweet potatoes to come pick sweet potatoes. God would make sure we had plenty. As harvest day grew closer, I was estimating that we might have as many as fifteen hundred people show up at our farm, ready to work.

As more and more people volunteered to help, the weather forecast for that Saturday grew more and more ominous. After a summer with hardly any rain, meteorologists were predicting a heavy downpour that day.

But I still had my faith! I was confident that if I did just the right things, I'd be able to move the hand of God in my favor. I started fasting on the Sunday before the harvest. I was going to have faith like potatoes, faith that could move mountains.

In reality, all of this "faith" was really just my own pride talking. I'd told everybody that First Fruits Farm would harvest 200,000 pounds of sweet potatoes this year. I had boasted. I had bragged. And even though I said it was all about God, it was about me, too, because I was the sweet-potato whisperer. I had a reputation to protect.

God knew I needed to be humbled.

All that week, despite all my prayers and all my fasting, the forecast barely changed. I clung to whatever hope I could. When the forecast on Friday said that the rain wouldn't really start until the afternoon, I rejoiced. *That won't be good for our harvest festival,* I thought, *but at least we'd have a good morning to actually do some harvesting.*

That Saturday morning, as more than a thousand people drove onto our farm and parked on the bare grass and dirt around our fields, I watched the blackest, heaviest, most ominous storm clouds roll in from the southeast. They were early.

"Hey, Jason," someone said, tapping me on the shoulder. "Looks like there's some really bad weather coming." He wasn't even looking at the clouds but rather at his phone. He was checking out the radar map, which had an angry dark-red patch—indicating a huge amount of rain—heading right toward our farm.

Sure enough, almost as soon as the last car of our more than one thousand volunteers rolled onto First Fruits Farm, the clouds opened up. It was as if the heavens had turned on a fire hose. It wasn't just a gentle North Carolina rain; it was a monsoon.

"Aaaaaahhhhhh!" came the screams from our volunteers. "Oh, Lord! It's raining!"

People were shrieking in terror, running for their cars as fast as they could, as if the sky were raining frogs. They cranked on their engines and tried to tear out of my makeshift parking lot, only by that time, the dirt underneath their tires was turning into sticky, slippery mud. For those who were trying to get out the fastest and revved their cars the highest, their tires churned the earth like a food processor, whipping the mud into a nice brown glue.

For a while, all I could do was just stand there, frozen in my rain slicker, as all my goals and hopes for the year were almost literally washed away.

I don't know if you remember the online Mannequin Challenge from several years back, where people would record themselves walking or sitting or dancing or whatnot and then suddenly stop, rooted in place as if they were made of stone. That was me that morning: frozen and speechless. I was rooted in place, looking like a mannequin with vacant eyes and open mouth, as the rain pounded down. I watched as all my volunteers ran in every direction imaginable, like crabs on the beach.

My farm. My crops. It's all going away.

Funny thing: the Wednesday night before, the youth-ministry pastor at our church had spoken on Gideon. In chapters 6 and 7 of the book of Judges, Gideon was called by God,

and the Lord promised him a huge victory over the Midianites.
But God wasn't going to give him the victory in a way that
might be misinterpreted as *Gideon's* victory, born of his own
strength. God thought that Gideon's twenty-two thousand
men were just too many, so He had Gideon whittle down his
forces until he had just three hundred men. And, sure enough,
God led the Hebrew commander to victory.

I thought about that as I watched more than one thousand
volunteers run in terror and flee First Fruits Farm. I wasn't left
with three hundred people; I was left with fifty.

The rain kept coming. I eventually shook out of my stupor,
pushed some cars out of the mud, and got to work. I could
barely keep my eyes open as the sludge splattered off my face
and shoulders. It was a cold rain, too, and the chill worked its
way under my rain gear and clothes and dug under my skin.
The fields were so muddy and sticky that our boots sank and
slid as we worked. It was, in so many ways, a miserable harvest
day.

But those fifty volunteers—those brave, hardy souls that
stayed—didn't seem to care. They were soaked to the bone,
just as I was. The mud sucked at their feet, just as it did mine.
They were, like Gideon's soldiers, the faithful few—the few
who remained of my volunteer army, who worked for hours in
the rain and cold. They weren't fighting Midianites; they were
fighting the rain. But more importantly, they were fighting
hunger.

Many of the remaining fifty were youth with Grace Christian Academy who had traveled all the way from Pennsylvania.
They taught me something about character that day. Those
young men and women, the faithful few who stayed, were the
sort of people you'd share a foxhole with. They were the sort
of people you'd want by your bedside if you were sick, who'd
mourn with you if you were grieving, who'd stay with you if

you were scared. I've heard the phrase *fair-weather friends* most of my life, and plenty volunteered that day. I don't want to diminish their desire to help in the first place; just signing up and showing up illustrated that their hearts were in the right place. But on days like that, you need the stomach for it too. But when the rains came and almost everyone left, those sweet potatoes still needed to be harvested. Farmers don't have the luxury of working only when the sun shines, and those fifty people who stayed understood that. They were my *foul-weather* friends that morning—friends you could count on when the world's coming down around your ears, like was happening to me that day.

It's my prayer that we'd all become *foul*-weather friends. So many people are in need. So many people are hurting and scared and sorrowful. If we call ourselves Christians, we're called to bear one another's burdens. Let's ask ourselves, How well do we come alongside someone and work shoulder to shoulder with him or her in the rain?

Those fifty volunteers—those faithful few—helped harvest the thirty thousand pounds of sweet potatoes—potatoes that wouldn't have gotten out of the fields otherwise.

That's it: a meager thirty thousand pounds. I had thought that we would've grown two hundred thousand pounds of potatoes. I told everybody that's what First Fruits Farm was going to do. I'd *bragged* about it. But despite doubling the land dedicated to the crop, I didn't grow even what I'd grown the year before. Not even *half* that. Barely even a quarter.

I felt like such a failure. I felt like everyone was going to laugh at me again.

But at the end of the harvest, I looked up to heaven—the skies now done with their weeping—and gave thanks.

"God, thank You for what You've allowed us to harvest here. Thank You for these thirty thousand pounds of sweet potatoes. You're the One who's going to make sure this food goes where it's needed. You're the One who's going to use these potatoes to feed the hungry, to give hope and encouragement to the poor. You're the One who provides the increase. That's not my responsibility. In faith, I know You're going to do the rest.

"And, God, forgive me for allowing my selfish pride to get in the way of this harvest, to get in the way of accomplishing Your will. Amen."

Harsh Lessons

I learned a lot of lessons that year. I learned never to boast— never to count your sweet potatoes before they're grown. I learned something about character, too, and that people of the truest, purest character—those foul-weather friends—are a rare and priceless find.

But maybe the biggest lesson I learned was this: God's criteria for success is very different from the world's.

One day not so long ago, Tay told me something pretty profound, something I sometimes forget, and something I wasn't even thinking about in 2015.

"There're so many people looking at us and our farm," she said. "So many people have all these different expectations for us. So many people are judging us based on our success. But you know what? That's them. We can't fall into that success trap, Jason, and we cannot be focused on setting our value on being successful farmers. That is the trap of the world.

"God hasn't called us to be successful," Tay continued. "God has called us to be *faithful*."

I think we all struggle to remember that sometimes. The world makes it easy to forget.

Most of our lives are driven by results. When I was in the

NFL, it didn't matter how hard you played or how skillfully you blocked or how exquisitely you snapped: in the end, it was all about wins and losses. Lose two or three games in a row, and the fingers start pointing. Blame starts flying. Lose four or five games? Six? Desperation sets in. I still follow a few of my former teammates on social media, and, man, if their team is having a bad year, their fans let them have it. They'll praise those players when everything's going well. But if you have a bad year, the people say, *We're going to shame you. You deserve it.* I can't emphasize enough how stressful that environment can be, how the pressure not only to do your own job well but also to make the team successful—even though you're only a fraction of that team—can eat away at you.

It's not just football. We're all about success in this culture. We're all about results. It doesn't matter so much if Junior *understands* fractions, as long as he gets an A on the test. It doesn't matter if Mary Jo loves playing the violin if she's not first chair in the school orchestra. Post a cute video but it doesn't get enough likes on Facebook or Instagram? Why did you bother to post it?

The Christian world is often no exception. Some pastors think that if their congregations aren't growing, they're failing God somehow. Or, on the flip side, pastors whose congregations *are* growing rapidly think it's because God is particularly pleased with them. Then what happens if the numbers start slipping? All of us are pushed to watch for tangible, quantifiable results. We can be slaves to our own success.

God knows something we forget: Behind every number is a person. Behind every statistic is a story. While the rest of us follow our spreadsheets, God—in His infinite understanding—can look beyond all that. He can use our failures as much as our successes, our disappointments as much as our victories.

Now, don't get me wrong: there are many people counting

on the food we grow here at First Fruits Farm. We have many people and organizations depending on us. I take that to heart, and we strive to be excellent in everything we do. We sow and grow our seeds in faith, and we try to give excellent attention to every little detail. We celebrate when we pull in a bumper crop, and we should, because it means we're able to feed more people.

But I remember Tay's words: I wasn't called to be successful. I was called to be faithful. I'm a farmer. I plant the seeds, care for them as best I can, and let God do the rest.

You weigh those sweet potatoes we harvested in 2015 and measure them up to our 2014 harvest, and that crop was a failure. Numbers don't lie. But if I had grown *three hundred* pounds of potatoes that year, not thirty thousand, and been sincerely following God that whole time—following in faith—would I be a failure in His eyes? I don't think so.

The Favor of God

That wasn't the last time we had a bad crop. We've had others since. But God has blessed us with bumper crops too. And sometimes we've had harvests that went right by the book. That's the life of a farmer. You push through the bad seasons, you celebrate the good ones, and overall they seem to even out.

To follow God in faith means to trust in Him, but He doesn't offer any guarantees that you'll always be comfortable or always be happy. Tests and trials are part of following God too. Failure is as well. People who say that to be a Christian is to be happy and wealthy all the rest of your days . . . well, it seems as if those people never read the Bible.

When God first called me to be a farmer, He kept bringing

me back to the story of Joseph. I'd read that story over and over again. God used it to plant seeds of His own in my life—seeds that grew thirty-, sixty-, maybe a hundredfold. But now that I've been a farmer for a while—now that I've had my share of financial and agricultural disasters—I look at that story a little differently.

Throughout Genesis 37–50, we see how God orchestrated Joseph's life in amazing ways. "The Lord was with Joseph," it says throughout the story. Preachers often say that he *found favor with God*. And you'd think that would've been awesome for him.

Hold on a second. You mean that when Joseph's brothers conspired against him and plotted to kill him, he had the favor of God? When his brothers sold him into slavery, he had the favor of God? Or what about when Joseph was serving in the house of that powerful Egyptian official Potiphar and he was falsely accused by Potiphar's wife and thrown in jail? That's the favor of God? Or when he was stuck in that prison for so many years? Or when he successfully interpreted the dream of Pharaoh's own cupbearer, and the cupbearer forgot to put in a good word for his old prison buddy? That's *favor*?

Joseph's story tells me that just because you're doing the will of God doesn't mean you'll be protected from life. It tells me that even if God has big plans for you, it doesn't mean you won't encounter suffering along the way. When we follow God, He won't always lead us through sun-dappled fields and beautiful hillsides. We'll go through valleys. We'll have to cross deep, dark places.

God is good, *all* the time. Can we still say that? Absolutely. But sometimes we have to get to the end of the story to see that goodness completely. Just like Joseph did.

I can feel Joseph. I can feel how he must've felt in prison. I can see the darkness. I can see the times when he feels like he's all alone. I can see the times when he feels that God has forsaken him.

But God was still with him. It's right there in the Bible: God was with him the whole time.

I am still tempted to make this story—my story, my wife's story, my family's story—all about *me*. I want to be selfish. But then, when I look at Joseph's story, I realize that it's not about me at all. It's about God's will being done. That's it. Not *my* will be done, not yours, but God's.

God knows that every sweet potato I grow goes to someone precious in His eyes, some part of His incomparable creation. Someone with his own story. Someone with her own part to play in God's own huge epic tale.

What if my whole work on the farm—my whole life—is to help just *one* of those stories along. Everything that we're doing right now, and everything we've gone through, could be just to help one family—a family that God is going to use in an awesome, incredible way. Maybe a little boy or a little girl in that family will grow up to do something amazing, and giving them a sweet potato that kept them going one day will be, in God's eyes, the most significant thing I've ever done.

Success is nice, but I wasn't called to be successful—at least not how the world defines it. I wasn't called to be comfortable. I was called to be faithful. I was called to follow God in determination and humility and deep, deep awe. It's God's job to make that faithfulness work out in the end—to take whatever I grow and use it for His own awesome purposes.

Isn't that what every Christian should be about? To follow? To forget about success and be as faithful to our calling as we can?

It's not about *me*; it's about *Thee*. Thy will be done, God. All the time.

CHAPTER 10

The Real Harvest

I was outside working when, from the house, Tay called me. "Jason, the baby's coming," she said.

"That's great!" I said. "I'll give the midwife a call, and she'll be here in a couple of hours, and—"

"No, Jason, you don't understand," Tay said. "The baby's coming *right now*!"

My stomach dropped to my ankles. "Right now?" I said. "Like *now* now?"

• • •

Tay and I have always believed in having babies as naturally as possible. When I was playing with the Baltimore Ravens and we were expecting our first, JW, we prepared and prayed over an awesome birthing plan. We shared it with the birthing team at the hospital, and they seemed fine with it.

But hospitals have their own worries. Even though women

have been giving birth for thousands of years, well before the first hospitals were built, it can be dangerous. Doctors don't want anything bad happening to mother and child, and they *certainly* don't want to be liable for anything that might happen. So, if something unexpected occurs, doctors and nurses tend to fall back on things they're familiar with. And that means drugs.

The unexpected happened with JW. The labor went on longer than any of us hoped it would, so the birth unit suggested that Tay accept some Pitocin, a drug that makes the contractions stronger and much more intense. Then, when Tay was really feeling those harsher contractions brought about by the Pitocin, they offered her an epidural—a strong painkiller that gets injected right into the patient's back. But those epidurals sometimes can impact the baby's own heart rate, and that's what we saw with JW. While he was still inside Tay, his heart rate dropped, so the doctor decided to perform an emergency cesarean section.

"Don't worry," the doctor said. "We've done this procedure countless times. Everything's going to be fine."

And it was. When JW finally decided to see the world, he came out as healthy as could be. He's twelve right now and the engineer of the family. He loves to tinker around and build stuff. He already drives everything we have on the farm—the truck, the tractor, the forklift, you name it—and it's in part so he can figure out how it all works. Even if you tell JW *not* to drive something, well, you better hide your keys. Just in case.

Still, the birth at the hospital felt very unnatural to us. And when our second child was due to be born while we were living in St. Louis, Tay and I were determined again to do it as naturally as we could. Again, the hospital thought that our birthing plan was just great. The staff was on board with everything we hoped to do, until it came time to give birth. Naomi's birth story was a carbon copy of JW's: for the second time, we were forced to do an emergency C-section.

Naomi is nine now, and an artist—like my brother was. Last year I bought her a sketch pad for Christmas and she'd filled every one of the pad's two hundred pages with art by the end of February. She draws beautiful scenes, especially of the farm: the barns, the silos, the trees and ponds. Whenever I need to send a special thank-you note to somebody, I ask Naomi to draw me a picture. I tell her who the card's to and what it's for; I tell her exactly what I need. And in thirty minutes, she'll have a beautiful card ready for me. She's like our home's very own Hallmark store.

Tay and I had always wanted at least three children, and we were determined this time to do the birth the natural way. But even though the second C-section didn't change our desire to birth our next baby more naturally, doctors and hospitals were skeptical. As we talked with doctors about our plans, none of them would take us on. To perform a vaginal birth after two emergency C-sections was, at the very least, unusual, they told us. And Tay's history made her too much of a risk to go a different route. *Her history suggests that a C-section is the best way to go,* they'd say.

We weren't going to do that again. Not if we could avoid it. If a doctor wouldn't help us through a more natural childbirth, we'd take matters into our own hands. We decided we would have the baby at home. We hired a midwife, not a doctor, and in December 2012, she helped bring Noah into the world, a very short time after we'd bought the farm itself. He was the first baby born there.

Noah has spent seven whole years on the farm now, and he's the household's little preacher. Sometimes he'll just stand up and start preaching to his little brothers and sisters as if he were in a church pulpit. *This is what Jesus said,* he'll say, and,

This is what Jesus did, and Noah *knows.* He knows the stories of Jesus backward and forward. He's the family bookworm too. We homeschool the kids, and every day we have time where they can go outside and play—recess time so they can burn off their excess energy and, once they're back inside, pay attention again. But Noah, even though he might be the child who has the most pent-up energy and needs recess time more than anyone, will try to work all the angles so he can stay inside and just read.

"Dad, can I stay inside and read my Bible?" Noah will ask.

"No, don't read your Bible!" I find myself telling him. "Go outside and play!"

I never thought I'd be telling any of my children to quit reading their Bibles, and I bet most Christian moms and dads would *love* it if their kids wanted to skip playtime to be in the Word. But you don't know Noah.

• • •

By 2014, the year Tay gave me that anxious call, she and I were mother and father to those three wonderful children. When it came to having babies, my wife was a seasoned pro by then.

I was not. Sure, I'd been *around* when Noah was born. I helped where I could. But Tay and the midwife did all the real work. It was a beautiful experience—*awesome,* in the truest definition of the word. But I appreciated the moment mostly on the sidelines, admiring the miracle of birth like an art connoisseur might appreciate a famous Renaissance sculpture, or like a fan in the stands might cheer an overtime win. It's all well and good to appreciate the process and celebrate the final product; it's another thing to actually help bring it about.

I was expecting my role to be much the same this time

around. Our midwife, though, knew that babies aren't that predictable. This baby might decide to show up when she wasn't there, or he might come much faster than expected. So, a couple of weeks before Tay went into labor, our midwife pulled me aside and handed me a small box.

She said, "Hey, Jason, just in case anything happens—if there's an emergency or something—let me give you this. There's some material in it that you should look over if I'm not here. Read it over. Get comfortable with it."

I smiled and nodded and thought, *Read it? Are you kidding? If I could do this myself, why would I be paying you? You'll be here. Everything'll be fine.* I pushed the whole conversation off to the side, and I didn't think of it again. Well, not until . . .

"The baby's coming *right now!*"

In that moment, as Tay was shouting at me over the phone that our fourth baby was on his way and that he was coming as fast as a runaway train, I came to a staggering realization: I was going to have to deliver this baby myself.

As gently and calmly as I could, I said, "Um, Tay, do you remember what you did with that birthing kit? All that material that I was supposed to read?"

Well, she told me, and I had to skim through all that reading in about fifteen minutes. I gave myself a crash course in delivering babies, reading the stuff that looked important, flying through the illustrations and feeling very unequal to the task of helping bring a new life into the world.

It took me more than a year to really learn how to bring sweet potatoes into being. Now I was going to have to deliver a child?

Tay had no confidence in me whatsoever. Her stress level was straight through the farmhouse's roof. The fact that I didn't know where the birthing kit was or that I hadn't read over what was in it didn't help Tay's trust in my abilities one little bit. And I couldn't blame her. She knew the truth: that I didn't really know what I was doing.

When I played football, everything we did during the week pointed to getting ready for a three-hour game. The coaching staff sometimes tried to make it feel as if those games were the most important three hours of our lives, and the preparation we underwent for those three short hours was unreal. Now, in what was *really* one of the most important moments of my life, I felt woefully underprepared. I didn't have a pregame meeting to go over the game plan. I didn't have a coach to help me work through the techniques. And that afternoon, I was definitely far more terrified than I'd ever been before going up against the Pittsburgh Steelers or the New England Patriots. This was *real*. I knew exactly what was on the line: the life and health of my child, and the health and safety of the wife I loved. This was my *family*.

So I did what I always do when I'm way out of my depth: I prayed.

"God, You know I have no idea what I'm doing," I admitted as I prepared for the birth. "So, God, I need Your help. I need You to anoint my hands. I need You to give me the wisdom right now. In my time of need, give me the strength and understanding I need to bring this little baby safely into our family."

After the prayer, I took JW and Naomi and Noah and sat them down at the table. I made their dinner as fast as I could and put it in front of them.

"All right, let's say our prayers and eat," I said. I led them in grace, smiled reassuringly, and went over to the kitchen sink and washed my hands like a surgeon. And then I walked, absolutely terrified, into the next room where my wife was in labor.

I tried to be as calm and assertive as I could. I reminded Tay of various breathing techniques, trying to coach her through the pain. I held her hand, wiped her forehead, and assured her that everything was fine, everything was great, everything was okay.

But on the inside, I was *freaking out*. I knew things were not okay *at all*, because I had *no idea what I was doing*!

"You're doing great, dear," I said. "Breathe. Use your breathing exercises." I needed some of those breathing exercises too. Our fourth child hadn't made his big debut just yet, but let me tell you, there was still a baby in that room—or, at least, some big farmer who inside was crying like one.

I went back in the other room to check on the kids.

Praise God, I thought. *They're all doing fine. No one's screaming, no one's crying, and no one's bleeding.*

"You're doing great!" I assured the children.

I called my mom and dad, who live just forty minutes away, and told them the glorious, terrifying news.

"He's on the way!" I shouted maybe a little too loudly.

And I went back in with Tay.

A few minutes later, I helped Tay into our bathroom, where we've got a big tub, and settled her in there. And right there—in our bathtub—I helped our son into our home, our family, our world.

After the delivery, my former sports agent, Harold, got wind of the story. And he either misunderstood the circumstances or, like some people, decided to embellish it a little.

"You remember Jason Brown?" I imagine him telling folks at parties. "The center? Played for the Ravens and the Rams? Had this crazy idea of becoming a farmer? Well, get this: *he delivered his own baby out in the middle of a meadow!*"

Nope, no meadow. Just a bathtub. I wasn't fending off coyotes or raccoons—just my own fear. But I think it makes for a pretty good story anyway.

We named him Lunsford Bernard Brown—in honor of my father, in honor of my brother. He's the third member of the Brown family who's borne that name, and because of that, we just call him Trey.

Babies

When Tay and I first met, one of our first conversations was actually about the number of children we wanted. Between three and five, we decided at the time. Ultimately, we combined those two numbers and now have an even eight: JW, Naomi, Noah, Kahlan, Trey, Judah, Olivia, and, as of December 2019, Isaiah.

That's a lot of children, and the world doesn't quite know how to handle families as big as ours. They don't make minivans big enough for ten people, so when we all go somewhere, we go in a big used church van. Obviously, we can't sit at a restaurant booth, so when we go out, we make due however we can, whether splitting up or squishing tables together. Even when Tay and I had just five or six children, people would actually stare at us as we walked down the street, pointing at us and counting up the kids as if we were a gaggle of geese with a bunch of goslings trailing behind.

But two or three generations ago, large families were the norm, especially those raised on farms and around agriculture. Men and women from those generations don't find it strange at all. They'll come up and tell me, "Oh, I was one of eight," or "I was one of twelve." We've met people who come from families of fifteen or even eighteen. I don't know if Tay and I will ever have that many kids. Even now, when we're practically halfway there, I can't imagine trying to raise eighteen children. But at the same time, if God blessed us with that many kids, we'd celebrate each and every one.

All our babies are so different from one another. Some people think that we have so many children that we wouldn't be able to keep track of them all. But Tay and I can't envision what life would be like without even one of them. God made each one so special, so unique, so *precious*.

You look at society today, and the preciousness of life often isn't valued as much as it once was. Life spans are certainly longer now than they were sixty or seventy years ago, but we've gotten stingy with giving that gift of life. Some people look at children as expenses: you pay to feed them, to house them, to pay for braces and dance lessons and college. The US Department of Agriculture says that the average family spends more than $233,000 to raise a child to age seventeen. And that's not even counting the emotional cost. Kids can try your patience too. They can break your heart. I understand all that. Tay and I are fully aware how much it costs to feed a big family every day, and our kids—as wonderful as they are—have given us plenty to worry and stress about. But what our babies give us in return—the value they bring to our family, the joy they've given Tay and me, the memories they've given each other—you can't put a return on that.

From where I sit here in my farmhouse—a farmhouse filled with all this love and laughter and, yes, noise and chaos and sometimes tears—I know that life is a *blessing*. Every single one of our children, with their characteristics and quirks and outsized personalities, is a treasure that can't be measured.

When you get to be a certain age, you start thinking about your legacy. What have you brought into the world? What have you given? Some people look at their career achievements or their bank accounts. Some have streets named after them. I think about the Ravens' stadium, now called the M&T Bank Stadium in Baltimore. A Ring of Honor circles the field, filled with the names of twenty or so Baltimore football greats (from both the Ravens and the old Baltimore Colts). Two statues stand outside the stadium: one of legendary Colts quarterback Johnny Unitas, and the other one of Ravens linebacker Ray Lewis. Many kids look at those statues or the names around that Ring of Honor and believe that's the kind of legacy they want: to have someone to think enough of you to stick your name in a stadium for everyone to see or to mold a hunk of bronze in your image.

All that stuff is great. But if you're really thinking about your legacy—what you want your memorial to the world to be—don't build a statue. Concentrate on your children. That's the sort of legacy the Bible holds dear. You can read Jesus's earthly genealogy all the way back to David, and then all the way back to Adam if you want. That shows how much the people of the Bible valued family—how much they valued the shared history that passes down from parents to children to grandchildren.

Families are complicated things, and not a one of them is perfect. But God's blessings flow through a family's veins just as surely as blood does. We're shaped and molded by our mothers and fathers, who were shaped and molded by theirs. And because of this, we're all influenced in some way by generations long gone. I never really knew my grandfather Jasper Brown. I never got to hear his stories. But who he was helped make me the man I am today. There's a piece of him inside me. And because his grandfather was a piece of his upbringing, there's a piece of him in me too.

Family is our real legacy. It's a big reason why Tay and I moved out here in the first place. We want to raise our kids with whatever wisdom we have to offer and give them whatever character we have to give. We didn't want to see them just at dinnertime. We didn't want to ship our babies off to school to be raised and taught by strangers. They're *our* children. We want them to grow up learning our values. We take our responsibility as parents seriously.

If ever I feel my focus on family falter, I think about something that Tay told me one day.

"Jason, we grow a lot of food on this farm," she said. "We help feed a lot of people, people we don't even know. We raise a lot of animals. We give a lot, and we're a blessing to this community. But don't you ever forget that the most important thing growing on First Fruits Farm is our *family*. The love between a husband and a wife. The love that we share with our children. *That* is the most important thing growing here."

You want to talk about being centered? Tay is centered, and she helps center me. She reminds me of what's important. She reminds me of where we were in St. Louis, when our bank accounts were full but our hearts were empty—when we had more money than we knew what to do with but not enough love for, or time with, each other.

Watering and Pruning

Most of our kids were born on the farm, so it's all they've ever known. Only JW has any memories of our lives before we came back to North Carolina. If he'd been older—if we had left St. Louis when he was twelve—he might've been sad to leave that old life, with its ridiculous mansion and luxury lifestyle and NFL-playing dad. If the popular culture had sunk its teeth into him then, he might've felt the pull of that life a little bit more. And, listen, I get it. It's very attractive. When I go out and give talks to schools, many of the children and teens I speak to can't comprehend giving up the life of a professional athlete for the life of a farmer. To them, it doesn't make sense. Some of them look at me as if I were crazy.

But JW was four at the time, and for him the farm wasn't a step down from wealth and security. It was a step up—a new adventure. *Wow! A real pasture! A real pond! Look at all this land!* What more could a boy want? And it's a life that not many children get to experience now. Many people have no idea how the food they see at the grocery store ever gets there or the work it takes to make it happen. Many have never even *seen* a farm. And because of that, with the right attitude, farming can feel as exciting as sailing on a pirate ship or blasting into outer space.

When JW was seven or eight years old, he and I were cleaning out some of the stalls in the barn. He was helping do a few little things, but I was doing most of the work, and *all* of the real dirty work: mucking all the animal poop out of the barn. It was heavy and filthy and smelled to high heaven.

He watched me work. He could see how hard it was. He could smell that loamy scent of animal poop, just like I could. But he still said, "Dad, can I do that? Please? *Please!?* I'll do a good job—I promise!"

He's begging me—literally *begging* me—to shovel poop.

"You mark this day down and don't forget it for the rest of your life," I told him. "The day you begged me to shovel poop out of the barn."

It was a good reminder to me of what a gift this farm is. More than that, it's a gift to be able to *work* on this farm. As adults, we forget about that sometimes. I look at all the work First Fruits requires of me, and I can think of it as drudgery. It feels like the punishment of Genesis 3:19, when God told Adam that "by the sweat of your brow you will eat your food"

(NIV). But even work is a gift, too, and sometimes our children remind us of that. And in that moment, when JW begged to muck out the stalls, I thought, *Why can't we all look at work with that kind of enthusiasm? Hey, it's got to be done anyway, right? Why not* enjoy *doing it?* Even today when I get weary and tired, I look at my children's enthusiasm they show for every day. They can be happy for no reason at all. That gives me encouragement. My children and their love of life give me extra fuel in the tank.

They love the farm too. They don't always love everything about it, and you never know how that will change as they get older. But they see the beauty of it, even as they do their own share of work. Maybe that work helps them see the beauty all the more. This place of sweat and toil can sometimes look like Eden to them. It looks like one of Naomi's beautiful pictures.

Naomi gets it. She's a step back in time. She would've been right at home on a farm in the 1920s, I think. Whenever anyone needs help in the kitchen, she's the first to volunteer. She loves to cook. She loves to clean. She loves to make things with her hands. Naomi already knows how to do some sewing and knitting.

I recently took some of our babies to the North Carolina state fair, and I think all the arts and crafts on display there—the variety and the quality—nearly blew her little mind. All the quilts, all the artwork, all the hand-carved crafts—it was incredible. I knew that Naomi was already plotting what her own booth would carry in the future. I tried to stoke that creativity.

We met a gentleman at the fair who makes amazing handwoven baskets from strips of wood he pulls from oak trees.

"Hey, I have oak trees on my farm!" I told him.

"That's great, because I need some new oak for my baskets," he said. "Would you be willing to barter? I'd give you a couple of my baskets right now if you'd let me come onto your property and get some wood."

"I don't want your baskets," I told him. "I want you to teach me and my daughter Naomi how to weave them."

This is an example of what the farm allows us to do. It's like a time machine back into the past. Most people, when they need something, just head out to Walmart or buy it on Amazon. Admittedly, we do our share of that too. But the farm gives us a window into simpler times, when people made more of what they needed. It helps us see and appreciate and even value self-sufficiency—the ability to create what we need all by ourselves. Very often what we create with our own two hands is more unique, more beautiful, and sometimes more functional than anything we could get at the store.

Our farm is practically self-sufficient now. Oh, we still buy plenty, but we don't have to buy that much extra food. After all, we don't just grow sweet potatoes. We raise chickens. We harvest fruits and vegetables. We even extract our own honey from the bees we keep on the property. Sure, putting on my white protective beekeeping suit makes me look a little like a marshmallow, but that's okay, because the fresh honey is delicious!

How many children have a chance to enjoy their own home-grown honey? That's an opportunity we never would've had if I'd stayed in the NFL. Making honey is not a fast process. Buying a plastic bottle of the stuff is certainly more convenient. But the process, just like much of what we do on our farm, teaches our children the real value of that honey—how hard the bees work to make it, how laborious (and fun) it is to extract it. And that makes that honey all the sweeter when they finally get a chance to taste it.

Like that honey, life on the farm is a little slower for our children, but a little sweeter. They're learning that doing their best means taking the time to do it right and do it well. They see the beauty and creativity that goes into the work here. Managing and growing things on a farm isn't just work; it's art.

No Boxes

When I think of those baskets that Naomi and I saw at the state fair, one thing's pretty obvious just by looking at them: every single one is different. These aren't manufactured by machine; they're crafted by a skilled hand, just like God crafts each of us. Some of the differences are due to design, but some of the more subtle variations come simply from the material they're made of. No strip of bark is exactly the same width or color or density, which makes each basket—even among baskets that are essentially the same size and shape—as unique and individual as fingerprints.

You look at our farm, and you see that God-given individuality everywhere. We have tons of the same kind of oak trees, but each one is still unique, shaped by its own environment and experience. All the millions of sweet potatoes we've grown might look the same at first glance, but no two are identical.

Children are the same way. That goes without saying, really. Any parent knows each child is unique. But in most places, that doesn't matter. We stick them all in the same box and expect them to thrive in the same environment. We have to. There's no way that one educational system, no matter how good or creative, can truly hone in on each child's individual needs and styles.

Because we homeschool our babies, and because we live way out in the middle of nowhere, we have the ability to tailor our children's upbringing in a way that not many parents or teachers can.

Take Noah, for instance—our little preacher.

Noah is *smart,* man. He didn't just memorize the Twenty-Third Psalm when he was four; he also learned how to read. When Tay was teaching Naomi how to piece together her ABCs and sound words out, Noah was in the same room, soaking it all in. He'd look at these books and listen to the lessons and puzzle many of those words out all by himself. When he was just five, I sat him down on my lap and tried to teach him a little something out of my old King James Bible. And *he* started reading it to *me*! I knew he was reading, not reciting something from memory, because when Noah would get to a word he couldn't pronounce (and there're a lot of them in the King James Version), he'd stop and work through it, syllable by syllable.

"Ne-buh-ke-ne-zer?" he'd say.

But he's also very energetic. If he were in a public school, they'd have a label for him, no question, and maybe a couple. "Hyperactive." "ADHD." You name it. And then they'd suggest some medication to calm him down.

I get it. When you're in a classroom catering to thirty other kids, you can't have one disrupting the class. You don't have time for special treatment.

But on the farm, when I see that Noah's getting particularly wriggly and not focusing on the lesson, I'll lead him to the back window.

"Do you see that tree out there?" I'll say, pointing to a solitary oak tree a quarter mile away.

"Yes, Dad."

"Noah, I want you to run to that tree and get me a leaf."

"Okay, Dad!" And he'll dash outside and get one for me.

When he returns, I'll say, "Noah, you tired yet?"

"No, Dad!"

"Okay, go back to that tree and get me another leaf!"

Sometimes he'll need to make that run three or four times, but he'll eventually say, "Okay, Dad, I'm tired now."

"Good," I'll say. "Now let's get back to our schoolwork."

It's the beauty of homeschooling. It's the beauty of living on the farm. We're able to treat each child individually, just as God made them. A teacher in a classroom just can't do that. As much as he or she might want to, the system doesn't allow it. Our kids, just like all kids, have different needs. They all learn in different ways. They all have different hopes and fears and problems, and they all respond to different motivators. Out here, we don't need to have a single, solitary box that all eight children have to fit in, as they've got a thousand-acre box to explore.

Bible Study

Our kids usually are up by six-thirty to do their chores. But in early 2018, I thought my oldest, JW, was ready to dive into some man-sized study. So I told him, "JW, I want you to be sitting down at the table by six on Monday morning."

Sure enough, he was there, and we started going over Proverbs. I wanted him to begin to understand the value of biblical wisdom and God's Word.

I wasn't showing favoritism. It was, if anything, an extra duty I saddled JW with. But Naomi and Noah didn't see it that way. All they saw was that JW was getting some special alone time with Dad. So, about a month later, they walked up to me and gave me a petition.

"Dad, we want to come to your Bible study," Naomi said.

"But it's so early in the morning!" I warned them.

"We don't care!" Naomi told me. "We want to come down and read the Bible with you too!"

"Are you sure?" I asked. I watched Naomi's and Noah's heads bob up and down.

"Well, all right!" I said. "The more the merrier."

So they started diving into the Scriptures with me too. Can you imagine? Kids clamoring to study the Word of God? They started soaking it up like a sponge, so much so that they eventually *kicked me out* of their little Bible study.

"Dad, we know you're busy," JW said. "We got this. If we have any questions, we'll ask."

I had mixed feelings about that initially, especially since my babies were so young. Running a Bible study by themselves? It's strange. And, because I know that they aren't going to be kids forever, I want to spend as much time with them as I can.

But Tay and I are grateful. It's like Proverbs 22:6 tells us: "Train up a child in the way he should go; even when he is old he will not depart from it." We're training our children in the Word of God, even if they're partially training themselves.

Here's the thing: children *should,* in part, train themselves. They need to learn stuff on their own. Parents are there to nurture and teach and push, but we also need to remember to let go at times. The best lessons—the most memorable lessons—aren't the ones you're read or told but the ones you experience for yourself.

Don't get me wrong: Tay and I protect our children from a lot of things. Our farm protects them from the dangers of city or suburban life. Our homeschooling protects them from teachings we don't approve of and helps guard them, to some extent, from some of the cultural hooks that sink into so many kids. And, as our children grow older, we'll have rules and guidelines to help deal with social media and dating and all the other perils that come with growing up. But the farm also allows our children to be children. They do their chores. They climb trees. They skin their knees, get into things they shouldn't, and, in JW's case, sometimes even drive the tractor when I say not to.

We don't want to be helicopter parents. On a farm this size, we need to be able to trust our children even when we can't see them. Eventually, all parents, no matter where they live, have to find a way to that same sense of trust. Children aren't children forever. They'll be out of your care quicker than you think, and they'll be forced to make their own decisions without your input. Sooner or later, you've got to let go. All parents do. Better to do it in stages, we feel. Better to give them a sense of both freedom and responsibility when they're still at home.

In 1963, just eighty minutes away from here, my grandfather Jasper Brown risked his life to offer his children better ones. He took them to a segregated school, hoping to give his children the sort of education that so many black children in the state were denied. Maybe his sons and daughters wouldn't have to be farmers. They'd have a choice.

He succeeded in that. He helped give them that choice. And, nearly fifty years later, his grandson *chose* to be a farmer. He chose to return to those roots made by Grandpa Jasper all those years before.

Education, as I think my grandpa knew, isn't just something you squeeze out of schools and books. Wisdom sure doesn't just come from a class. Oh, we don't skimp on knowledge on First Fruits Farm. Our children are getting what I'd consider a first-class education. They're learning things that most kids today will never even have the chance to experience: how to milk cows, how to drive tractors, how to extract honey from heavy, sticky honeycombs. And, through those chores, they learn lessons they don't necessarily know they're even learning. They are taught what it takes to grow food and what it means to work hard. They see the beauty and logic of God's creation all around them and how bountiful He's provided for us. They see in Tay and me, hopefully, what it means to be a mother and father who love and sacrifice and discipline and raise children in God's Word.

Tay once told me that the most important thing growing on First Fruits Farm is our family. She's absolutely right. Thanks to God, it's been a bumper crop so far.

Dana and Lunsford with their mom, Deborah, holding Jason.

Lunsford, Jason, and Dana.

Jason with his siblings and dad.

Jason, his parents, and his siblings prepare for a riverboat cruise in New Orleans, Louisiana.

Lunsford with Jason, who had just lost his two front teeth.

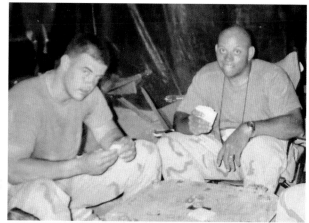

Lunsford (right) with an army friend, playing cards—one of his favorite hobbies.

Tay, Jason, and Jason's mom, Deborah, at Jason's final college home game.

Jason and JW celebrate Tay's UNC dental school graduation.

The Brown family pose for Jason and Tay's ten-year vow renewal.
© Gina Kropf

Four generations:
Grandpa Willie B. Jefferson
with Bernard (Jason's dad),
JW, Jason, and Noah Brown.

Jason proudly holds his first
bounty of cucumbers, gleaned
with the help of faithful
volunteers from the
Society of St. Andrew.

The Brown family in front of the miracle tractor.
© *Jamie Thayer Jones*

Jason and Tay.
© *Jamie Thayer Jones*

The Brown family and
their broccoli.
© *Jamie Thayer Jones*

The Browns gather for an annual front porch photo.
© *Jamie Thayer Jones*

The Brown family, including newborn Judah and both sets of grandparents, in front of the barn.
© *Jamie Thayer Jones*

When the deer don't get to the sweet potatoes, they can grow as big as a person's head.

Tay's bright smile fills the barnyard as she holds her goat Patty-Rona.

The Brown bunch pose for an Easter photo.
© Jamie Thayer Jones

The eight Brown family kids.
© *Jamie Thayer Jones*

The Browns at First Fruits Farm.
© *Jamie Thayer Jones*

CHAPTER 11

Dirty Miracles

I needed roosters. And it was all Bernard's fault. Bernard had just graduated from high school the year before. He came to First Fruits in 2018 as a lanky eighteen-year-old from Pennsylvania, ready to work for us for the season before going to college. He was a nice young man and a good worker. But he was a *great* eater. This was where Bernard's talents really lay. In the years before Bernard came to the farm, we'd cook a dozen eggs for breakfast—enough for all of our six (at the time) egg-eating children. But when Bernard came, we discovered that he could polish off a dozen eggs all by himself.

By Good Friday that year, I knew we had to come up with a way to find more food without *buying* more food. Specifically, we needed more laying hens. But, of course, for our hens to lay hatching eggs, we needed roosters to fertilize them. Two roosters would do, I figured. A couple of roosters meant more eggs and more chickens. And, with Bernard staying with us a few more months, a few more chickens might come in handy. If he got too hungry, we could toss him a couple of chickens before he started eating the bark off the oak trees.

I didn't know where we were going to find roosters, but I made up my mind that that's what we needed. I offered up a very simple prayer. Nothing tearful, nothing dramatic—just a straight, quick petition to the Lord.

"God, please help me find a couple of good roosters. Amen."

We went into town not long after to support a Good Friday cookout hosted by a tractor company. But as we made the ten-minute drive back to First Fruits Farm in our old church van, I saw a couple of birds loitering near the side of the road. *Could they be buzzards?* I wondered as we got closer. No, completely the wrong shape. *Chickens, maybe? Were we going to, at long last, learn why chickens really do cross the road?* No, they seemed too big for that. Whatever they were, though, they were standing right outside our farm, partly hidden in the thicket. It was almost as if they were caught there in the brush—just like a ram. Their feet looked as if they were practically on our property line.

Could they be . . .

I asked Tay, who was driving the car, "Do you see those?"

"See what?" Tay said.

"Those two roosters!"

Now, obviously, we live in the country. It's not like it's unusual to spot animals out here. We've seen plenty of wildlife on our way to and from town: dogs, cats, raccoons, deer, even snakes. But never, *ever*, had I seen a stray rooster, much less two.

Tay stopped the van. There in the brush, I saw an answered prayer. These weren't just any roosters either. They were Copper Marans—beautiful, proud, lean birds with black bodies and rust-colored necks and a bright-red comb on the tops of their heads.

I said, "JW, those are *roosters,* right? They aren't any of our chickens, are they?"

"No, Dad," he said. "They're definitely roosters. And we don't have any roosters."

"*Yes we do!*" I shouted. "I *prayed* for those roosters! God *blessed* us with those roosters! And now *we're gonna get those roosters!*"

I told JW and Bernard to hop out of the van and grab the birds before they waddled away. "Bernard, you better not let them go or else I'm sending you back home!" I hollered.

He didn't let them go. We brought them home, and I was thrilled. I took pictures of the birds. I posted those pictures on social media, praising God's provision as I did so. I celebrated the discovery of those roosters maybe more than I would've whooped it up after a playoff victory. This, I knew, was God's doing. These birds were meant for First Fruits Farm.

A friend of mine advised caution—that I shouldn't count my roosters before they hatch, so to speak.

"Listen, I know God blesses you in some strange ways, all right?" he said over the phone. "But if you're not careful, other people might see these roosters differently. While you're calling them a blessing from God, they'll think you're just a crazy Christian who stole somebody else's lost roosters."

I could see his point. I sure wouldn't want anyone to think that I'd gotten these roosters through "fowl play." After I got off the phone with him, I called up the local animal shelter and reported my find. I said that I'd just go ahead and hold those roosters for the owner until he or she claimed them; I'd feed them and give them water and make sure they were well taken care of.

"So, if anyone comes in looking for a pair of Copper Maran roosters, you can send them out to First Fruits Farm to claim them," I said.

"Sounds good, Mr. Brown," the lady on the other end of the phone told me. "And, if no one reports those missing roosters after thirty days, they're yours."

"I *know* they're my roosters!" I blurted. "God *gave* me those roosters! No one's going to contact you, because those roosters are *mine!*"

"Um . . . yes, Mr. Brown," the lady said. "We'll let you know. God bless. You have a nice day."

Stranger Things

No one claimed those roosters, of course. They're still out there in our chicken coop, helping us make eggs for our family and anyone else who might come for breakfast. Their arrival felt like a little miracle.

I should've gotten used to those sorts of miracles by now.

Our God is an awesome God. He can do anything. He is with us.

For many Christians, those are just words, even when we mean them. Most of us believe it, and we believe it with all our hearts. We know we worship an almighty ruler, the maker of heaven and earth. We say that He loves us and is involved in our lives. We say we depend on Him for everything.

But do we ever see it? Do we ever put it to the test? Or is it like me when I was in the NFL: worshipping God with my lips but putting my *real* trust in my bank account? We love God if it doesn't cost us too much. We'll put our trust in Him as long as we've got a couple of backup plans in place.

And you know what? I wonder whether our lukewarm love and half-hearted trust keeps many of us in a kind of spiritual shelter. We praise God from the safety of four walls. We look through a window at the world God intended for us. All the sights and sounds of life that God meant for us to experience and enjoy—the sun, the rain, the snow, the sorrow and joy and amazement—we keep safely away from us. Like those volunteers who ran to their cars on my farm during that 2015 harvest, we don't want to be bothered by the risk of rain.

But when we don't risk, we don't reap the rewards, either.

When you follow God—truly follow Him, body and soul—new doors seem to open up. You may find, as I have, that God really *is* with us and that He's an awesome God indeed. To trust Him—to open up the door and walk outside—leaves you vulnerable. The rains may come. But you know what? You feel the warmth of God's love on your face too. And sometimes those showers you feel? They're the showers of blessings.

God blesses you in some strange ways. That's what my friend told me when I first received those roosters. He added this: *You shouldn't be surprised, seeing miracle after miracle.*

Tay and I have indeed seen miracle after miracle on First Fruits Farm, beginning with the ability to buy the farm itself. I could fill a whole book with stories of these miracles. Here's another.

• • •

It was February of 2016 and I needed a greenhouse—a greenhouse to get our vegetable garden growing even while there was still the threat of frost. As it was, Tay and I were spending a ridiculous amount of money on starter tomato and pepper plants. If we had a greenhouse, we could start thousands of little seedlings and, in the long run, save some of what little money we had.

But in this case, it takes money to save money. Greenhouses

are expensive. The kind of greenhouse I needed *started* at $20,000. The ones I wanted were closer to $30,000. So I scrapped the idea of buying a new one and started looking for something used.

Not long after, I drove by and noticed an old unused greenhouse on a neighbor's property. The clear plastic covering for the structure was almost entirely destroyed. Trees were growing through the holes. The whole building was surrounded by weeds and brush. But the frame seemed to be in decent shape, and I wondered whether this was the greenhouse God meant for us.

I stopped by and talked with the man who owned the dilapidated greenhouse, and I offered him most of what Tay and I had to spend: $2,000.

He wanted $3,000. Just, essentially, for that used frame.

I went home and talked with Tay about it.

"Tay, I think God wants us to have a greenhouse," I told her. "Maybe we can find a little more money to buy this one."

"If God wants us to have a greenhouse, it's *not* this one," she said. "God has something better in store for us."

Months went by. The winter rolled on. It was then March, about time when we'd be starting our seedlings . . . if we had a greenhouse.

One day I went off to speak at a pep rally at a nearby middle school. After I finished my speech, I spent a few minutes talking with the school's athletic director. We talked about sports, of course, about baseball and football for a little while, and then he mentioned that some of the schoolkids were interested in farming and agriculture. In fact, he added, a few of them were working on a little greenhouse behind the school.

"Oh, that's awesome," I said. "My wife and I are in the market for a greenhouse."

That's all I said. I didn't say, "Hey, we are in serious need of a greenhouse." I didn't say, "We've been praying for a greenhouse." And I certainly didn't say, "We can't really afford a greenhouse, so it sure would be nice if someone would give us one." I simply said that we were in the market for one.

The next words out of his mouth were these: "Really? That's interesting. You know, when we bought our home four years ago, the previous owner built this state-of-the-art greenhouse in the backyard. We're not doing anything with it. Would you like it?"

I was shocked—so shocked, in fact, that I didn't even know how to receive the offer.

"No sir," I said finally. "That's very kind of you, but we couldn't take that kind of gift from you."

"No, you don't understand," the athletic director explained. "I've been just storing junk in it for years. My wife wants me to build an aboveground swimming pool right where the greenhouse stands. She wants it *gone*. Take it and you'll be doing me a favor."

When I went to look at it, I realized the greenhouse was way better than that old skeleton of one that my neighbor wanted to sell to me for $3,000. It was even way better than those $20,000 to $30,000 new greenhouses I'd been looking at. This greenhouse was a state-of-the-art commercial-grade $100,000 structure—a combination of everything I needed, everything I wanted, and some things I'd never dreamed of.

"How soon can I have it?" I asked.

"Immediately."

• • •

Those moments remind me that God is with us—that He's with us always. They help keep me moving forward. Because, trust me, this life hasn't been all miracles. Following God is costly too.

But here's the thing: if following God weren't so costly, we never would've seen most of those miracles.

Think about it: If my fortune was left intact, I would've just *bought* one of those $30,000 greenhouses. If I had still been a wealthy man, I would've just bought a new tractor. If I still had the resources I'd had in 2012, do you think I would've been excited about seeing a couple of roosters near my driveway?

In Matthew 17:24–27, Jesus and Peter are in Capernaum one day and Peter discovers they need to pay a tax. Jesus asks Peter how much the tax is, and Peter tells Him. So Jesus commands Peter to go down to the sea and cast his line out. "Take the first fish that comes up, and when you open its mouth you will find a shekel," Jesus says. "Take that and give it to [the tax collectors] for me and for yourself" (verse 27).

Now, in the Bible, this is almost a throwaway little miracle. Jesus seems so nonchalant about it, like it happens every day. But if you look at it from Peter's perspective, it's mind blowing. He's been a fisherman all his life. He's probably caught thousands upon thousands of fish in his career, maybe millions. I bet he'd *never* found money in a fish's mouth before. But there it is, just like Jesus told him.

If Peter were rich, would that miracle have taken place? Wouldn't he just have taken a shekel right out of his own bank account? If Peter's pockets were heavy with coins, would he ever have had a chance to be amazed?

But Peter didn't have a shekel. He needed a miracle. He needed God to help him out, because he had no other choice.

That's the type of faith that Tay and I have to have.

Ever since First Fruits Farm began, we've had no idea how we were going to make it work from year to year, sometimes even from week to week. We don't really have the resources to do what we're doing. Anyone with any financial sense would look at our plans—plans we believe come straight from God—and then look at our bank accounts and say, "This doesn't add up. How do you expect to fix the barn [or clear the field or buy a greenhouse] with what you have? How's that going to happen?"

Tay and I look at each other and say, "By God's grace." Our resources may be paltry, but we're tied to a kingdom with unlimited wealth and to a generous Father. That doesn't mean we squander what we have. We need to be good stewards of our resources. Those resources, no matter how well we manage them, are never enough to do what God has asked us to do.

But you know what? Everything we feel He's asked us to do, and everything for which we've gone to Him in prayer, has come to pass. *Everything.* Every vision. Every promise. Tay and I never have any idea how it's going to be accomplished. Or even when. But without exception and without fail, it happens.

When you look at the Bible, not many of its stories focus on rich people. If God's own plans were governed by spreadsheets, you'd think Jesus would've surrounded Himself with rich disciples who could fund His travels, not poor fishermen who couldn't pay their taxes. Joseph's family was probably relatively wealthy back in the day, but it was only when they were poor—when Joseph's brothers came to Egypt literally begging for food—that they had a chance to see Joseph's own amazing, miraculous story. Don't misunderstand: God uses rich people too. He used them in biblical times, and He uses them now. But the poor have a chance to see God operate more powerfully and intimately. They lean on Him because they don't have their own resources to use as a crutch.

Losing my fortune was painful. Tay and I still feel that pain. And I'd be lying to you if I said that sometimes we wouldn't love to have it all back. We could do some amazing things on First Fruits Farm with it.

But in the last several years, I've learned that having favor from God is worth more than gold and silver. Having that favor—having a real relationship with Him—is priceless, because God is always batting a thousand.

I know what it's like to have a big bank account. I know what it's like to live a comfortable life. But I'd never want to go back. I would much rather be in the position I'm in right now: praying to God every single day for my manna, praying for my daily bread. I don't need an abundance; just give me what I need.

The Man Box

I needed a forklift. I'd borrowed one in 2015 to move around all the sweet-potato boxes we needed for that year's harvest, but we couldn't do that every year. The First Fruits Farm needed its own. But, as usual, I didn't have the money for one. Forklifts, even used ones, can cost anywhere from $20,000 to $40,000. I had just $5,000 to spend on one.

I turned to Craigslist and found one for sale—one that seemed, from the ad, to be in decent condition—for just that amount. Praise the Lord, I said to myself, but there was a catch: it was all the way up in Richmond, Virginia, about 140 miles away.

So I called my dad, who owned a trailer capable of hauling the forklift back to the farm. "We're going on a road trip," I told him.

It's a long drive, so my dad and I prayed over everything: the truck, the trailer, the road, the people *on* the road, everything. We drove up to Richmond and arrived at the forklift owner's shop around midday. We greeted each other, and almost immediately the guy started talking about his "man box."

"Man box?" I asked. I'd never heard of a man box before. Never in my entire life.

The forklift seller showed us his own man box—essentially a metal platform with safety rails around the edges. Think of the bucket that workers from the phone company or power company use and combine that with what a scaffolding platform might look like, and you have a pretty good idea of what a man box looks like and how it works. The forks in the forklift fit in some slots underneath the box, and the forklift can then securely raise and lower the box so that the user can work in some high, difficult-to-reach places. It's safer than a ladder and far easier to work from.

It's a pretty ingenious contraption, and I could see all sorts of uses for it on the farm. I weighed just a little more than four hundred pounds at the time, and ladders and I don't get along that well. In fact, there's not really a ladder out there—even the heavy-duty ones—that has a weight limit that technically makes it safe for me to climb. I still used ladders, because you *have* to use ladders on the farm. But every time I climbed one, it was a risky adventure, like white-water rafting without a life jacket. So, every time I'd climb a ladder, I'd sing praise-and-worship music. I'd say to God, *I know there's no way You're going to allow me to fall or let this ladder break while I'm singing praises to You.*

But the man wasn't selling his man box, and I probably couldn't have afforded it even if he were. But I did take pictures of it from every angle. I knew a welder, and I figured maybe he could help me build one.

I bought the forklift, and my dad and I loaded it up on the trailer. We headed back home and eventually turned onto a gloomy two-lane highway that felt completely deserted for miles and miles.

We were right in the middle of Dinwiddie County, Virginia, when *pop*! A tire blew on the trailer. I didn't have a spare.

God, didn't I pray over the trailer? I asked internally, kind of furious that He would allow something to go wrong in the middle of nowhere like this. *Didn't we have this worked out?*

I pulled over to the side of the road, yanked out my phone, and started looking for somewhere, anywhere, that I might find a place to fix the tire. Good news: I found a tow-service facility about ten miles down the road. I didn't really want to spend the money to pay for a tow. It was money that I didn't have. I'd just spent $5,000 on a forklift, after all. *Maybe I can just limp another ten miles and get it to the service station myself,* I thought.

That was a mistake. By the time we got there, around five, I'd worn out the rim on the wheel too—another huge expense. This forklift was getting more expensive by the minute.

The towing facility looked practically deserted—the sort of place you'd see in a post-apocalyptic zombie movie. The place needed paint. I could see a junkyard out back. The sign in the window of the facility's shop area said it was open, but no one came out to greet us.

I said, "Dad, I'm going to go in and see if I can get us some help."

I walked in, and I found half a dozen guys in there—white guys—in dirty, greasy work clothes and overalls, slurping down spaghetti. One had sauce dripping down his chin. Some turned to stare at me when I walked in. A couple of them, including the guy who looked to be the man in charge, didn't even bother to do that. No one said hello. No one asked if I needed help.

Now, look, I'm not one to pull out the race card, but I was in the middle of rural Virginia. These men, by the looks of them, seemed like they might be the sort of folks who wouldn't be all that friendly toward someone who looks like me. And here's the thing: this service station was the only place for miles around. My dad and I were stranded there, at the mercy of those men. If something went wrong, there was nowhere to run. Nowhere to go.

I thought of my grandfather Jasper.

The man who looked like the man in charge kept chewing his spaghetti, and I saw him look at my truck and trailer out of the corner of his eye.

"That's a nice-lookin' forklift you got on that trailer," he said in his Virginia drawl. "How much you want for it?"

"Um, it's not for sale," I said. I tried to muster a smile. "In fact, I just bought it. I just need some help with fixing a flat."

He took another bite of spaghetti. He chewed it. Slowly.

"All right," he said finally. "Lemme finish my supper. I'll be out in a minute."

I smiled, said thanks, and walked—*backward*—through the front door and toward the truck, keeping an eye on the men all the way. *God, please,* I said silently. *Please, please, please, help me.*

My dad looked at me through the truck window. "Is everything all right?"

"Dad, just—just stay in the car," I told him. "Lock the doors and don't say anything, okay?"

The man—the leader—sauntered out of the building, rubbing his hands on his clothes.

"Sure ya don't want to sell that forklift?" he drawled.

I was scared. Me, a four-hundred-pound ex–football player, terrified.

"I can't, I'm afraid," I said, forcing the nerves out of my voice. "Like I said, I just bought it. I have a farm in North Carolina, and I need it. For my fruits and vegetables and stuff." And then, just to make conversation, I said, "Yeah, and I'm going to make a man box for it. Just found out what one was today."

The guy looked me over again. Then he turned to his service station and pointed.

"See that metalwork up there?" he said. "Did all that from a man box. Made it myself. Yep, they sure come in handy. Yeah, that ole man box, it's sitting on top of a junk pile out back. Ain't had any use for it since."

And then he added, "Tell you what. After I get your wheel all fixed and your tire all patched, we'll load that man box up in your trailer. You can just take it home with you."

My jaw dropped. Just hours before, I hadn't even known what a man box was. Now I owned one. Not a *minute* before, I was a little worried my dad and I wouldn't even make it back on the road. Suddenly, I was a man box richer—and more mindful than ever to never judge things, or people, too quickly or too harshly. This was the last person that I would've expected to help me—that God would've used to bless me. But I drove out of that place deeply blessed.

I'd been angry that God had let my tire blow in the middle of nowhere. And, when I finally reached the place that might fix that tire, I felt abandoned. Forsaken.

I should've known that God orchestrated the whole trip. What looked like a disaster turned out to be a blessing.

In a way, that's the story of First Fruits Farm too. What looked like a setback was just another step toward something wonderful. What felt like a disaster brought us into a place of peace and trust and opened the door for miracles.

Dirt

First Fruits Farm, when you get down to its bare essentials, is just a thousand acres of dirt. Oh yeah, drive by and you'll notice it's filled with plenty of other things: trees and ponds and barns and crops. The dirt might be the last thing you see. And that's not surprising. To most people's eyes, dirt's not much to look at. It's brown and boring. Get dirt on your hands, and you scrub it away with soap and water. Get mud on your shoes, and you scrape it off. We don't like dirt. It's messy. It's filthy. When we say that someone treats you like dirt, it's no compliment. Dirt is about the lowest, humblest material on God's green earth. But put a seed in that dirt and give it a little sun and water and care, and it grows into something useful, even beautiful.

We're made of dirt, according to the Bible. "God formed the man of dust from the ground," it says in Genesis 2:7. And what does God do? He takes us and plants a seed in us. He molds us in His own image.

Sometimes when we look around the landscape of our lives, we see something dirty. Ugly. We see failures and disasters and setbacks. We look at those grimy moments in our lives and wish we could just wash them away. But God uses those moments to grow something good. Something awesome and true. Something miraculous. He uses humble people, and people who've been humbled, to do great works for Him and His kingdom. But we have to trust Him. We have to allow Him to work through us, even if sometimes it can feel painful.

I look around our farm and think about how good, and how generous, our God is sometimes. How even during the darkest of times—those times when our finances were such that we could barely pay our bills—God sustained us through it all.

How He blessed us when we needed it, how He gave us strength and courage when we felt as though we couldn't take another step in this life. I look at all the miracles He's given us. I'm not talking about tractors or greenhouses or man boxes; I'm talking about our children. Our family. Our love for each other. I look at my new baby, Isaiah, and I know what a miracle he is.

I needed roosters. I needed a greenhouse. I needed a forklift.

But what do I really need? What has been the only thing I've ever needed? God. Just God.

CHAPTER 12

Feast

I worked hard when I was in football. I practiced and played through some sweltering days. I've seen fellow players almost faint from the work and heat. But nothing I've ever done in the sport—no game, no two-a-day practice—prepared me for picking cucumbers in June.

I mentioned earlier how I connected with the Society of St. Andrew, a network of volunteer gleaners, who helped harvest my very first crop in 2014 (and still harvest at First Fruits Farm today). I talked about how I connected them with my friend Len Wester and they gleaned his cucumber fields that summer, gathering more than ten thousand pounds.

I was one of those volunteer gleaners that late June day. I was combing Len Wester's fields for leftover cucumbers—bending down again and again, over and over.

I wasn't that far removed from my football days, but I wasn't in gleaning shape. It wasn't too long before I started to feel the wear of all that bending. I could feel the twinge in my lower back muscles—pain that kept growing and growing with each new move to grab another cucumber. It wasn't long before it was just this sharp pain radiating all through my lower back. Then, as I kept pushing those muscles harder and harder, they eventually started to just lock up.

That happened to me in thirty minutes. I was supposed to be out there for two hours.

And I was. I pushed through all that pain, through the seizing muscles in my lower back. I worked alongside nearly a hundred volunteers who, surely, were hurting just as much as I was. None of us were getting paid for this work. We'd *volunteered* to suffer like this. We'd given up a perfectly fine Saturday morning. That work tests your commitment. It tests your strength. It even tests your faith.

But when I stood up, stretched my back out as much as I could, and looked around at the gleaners in the field, I saw something pretty inspiring: the awesome quality of people who'd volunteer to do something like that. I knew what they'd given up. I knew they had to have a passion for what they were doing—a passion to help and feed needy communities. I saw the real quality of people then, people I'd want to be friends with, people I'd want in my inner circle.

I was exhausted. I was in pain. But I knew I was doing something worthwhile with good people. And that was pretty awesome.

Worn and Weary

A man once asked me what Tay and I enjoy most about the farm. I could've said so many things, because we enjoy a lot about our lives. But when he asked me, I hesitated for a moment. The truth is, Tay and I are still trying to find a sense of balance in our lives here. We're still trying to find that peace and joy, but often it's hard to do so with such a demanding and laborsome lifestyle.

We've found love here, for sure. We've found purpose on First Fruits Farm. But in the middle of feeling that love and purpose, I'm often exhausted. The sweat I put into football is nothing compared to what I've watered these fields with. I look at our house, and I think that someday I'll be able to enjoy it. I'll be able to sit down and truly *relax*. In August, I sometimes fantasize about being lazy come January, when there's nothing to plow or pick or harvest. But even in the winter, Tay and I work just as hard. We're still getting after it.

God tells us that He'll never give us more than we can handle. But sometimes, between the work and the financial stress and wrangling eight children, it feels like we *can't* handle it. Tay and I can feel so tired from it all—tired to the point where it feels like we might break. And the demands never stop.

Tay is often overlooked in our ministry. And some of that is just natural, as I'm the ex–NFL player, the guy who speaks to churches and schools. Tay doesn't like to be the center of attention. But sometimes people will push by Tay to talk to me, or they'll call us up and treat her like a secretary. They don't know how disrespectful that is. They don't know that she's the glue that holds it all together. She's the one who pushes me when I need pushing, who comforts me when I need comforting, who grounds me when I need grounding. She's the one who keeps me centered.

But she struggles too. I pulled her with me on this journey, remember—this crazy call of God. And sometimes it's up to me to help her.

Tay reads every email that comes to First Fruits Farm, and many of those emails come with some pretty unique requests. People know that we donate almost everything we grow. But they don't know how much Tay and I have struggled financially over the last several years. As a result, people often write in and ask us for *financial* help. We've had people ask us for houses, for cars, and to help pay someone's college tuition. A church asked us one time to cosign on a million-dollar mortgage.

For me, it's easy to just let those requests go by. I know what God called me to be. He called me to be a farmer. I'm not a bank. Even if I had the money, I can't give it to everyone who asks.

But Tay's heart is so sympathetic. She reads those emails and feels the need behind them. That sort of tenderness is a gift—but it can be a curse too. She tries to prayerfully answer every email we get. She tries to really consider each and every one. I've seen her sit at the computer, literally all day, looking at just one email, praying and agonizing over it.

"I don't know how to respond to this person," she'll say, and she'll detail whatever wildly expensive request they're making.

"Well, that's easy!" I tell her. "We can't help them!" We don't have the money.

"Look, we're doing what God has called us to do," I tell her. "We're farming. We're growing food. I know the world has countless other causes. There are so many people and organizations that really do need money. They need resources. They do need a blessing. But we've got to focus on what God called us to focus on. We've got to do what God called us to do."

That's enough for now. Honestly, sometimes it feels like too much.

Hard Blessings

To be a Christian means to follow Christ—and to follow His example all the way to the cross. If someone asks for our coat, we're to give him our shirt too. We're to give freely and cheerfully, to sacrifice for others as Jesus did for us.

Give, God tells us. *Give till it hurts.*

It's been hurting for a while now.

During that first harvest in 2014, we saw how great the need was—how much hunger there was, even in our little area of North Carolina. We knew we had to keep giving.

First Fruits Farm has truly become, in practice, *All* Fruits Farm. Except for what we hold back for ourselves and our children, we give the food we grow away. Food banks and soup kitchens depend on what we grow. We've donated more than a million pounds of food since we started First Fruits Farm; we've fed countless families. But it hasn't been easy. We've wondered sometimes how we'd be able to keep doing what we're doing.

People have told us that what we're doing is not sustainable— that we can't keep giving away everything we grow and hope that the miracles will still keep coming.

"You keep giving help like this," my father sometimes tells me, "and pretty soon, *you're* going to be the one who needs some help."

He's got a point. But I also recognize that I'm attached to a kingdom with unlimited resources—that I'm loved by a generous God. And so we keep giving. We keep working. We keep doing what God called us to do.

I'm working harder now than I ever did playing football. I'm sacrificing more now than I ever did playing football. And some people might wonder, *Why bother? Why put so much into this work when, compared to the NFL, you're getting so little out of it?*

But here's the difference between my life then and my life now: When I go to bed, I have a sense of peace and satisfaction. The stress that I felt playing football is gone. And, although it's been replaced by different stresses, I know that all my problems come with a purpose. A mission. I know that what I'm doing now isn't just for me. It isn't even just about all the thousands of people who might otherwise go hungry. It's for *God*.

I'm doing what God has truly called me to do. Football? The NFL? That just helped prepare the way.

One of the Bible's most famous verses is Philippians 4:13: "I can do all things through Christ who strengthens me" (NKJV). Sometimes when you hear ministers preach on that verse, they concentrate on the "I can do all things" part. "I can do *all* things!" they say, and they talk about the miracles that the disciples and apostles performed: healing the sick and curing the paralytic and even raising the dead.

But you know what? The context in which Paul said that has nothing to do with great, miraculous happenings. He was talking about being strong through difficult circumstances and finding a sense of contentment even in the midst of them. Paul was saying, *Look, I know what it feels like to be hungry. I know what it feels like to be full. I know what it feels like to be rich, and to be poor. But I've learned how to be content in every state.* "I can do all things through Christ who strengthens me," Paul said. That's where the stress should be. Paul wasn't talking about miracles; he was talking about finding peace through God's plan, even when that plan is hard.

I know what it's like to be rich, and to be poor. I know what it's like to have everything, and I know what it's like to cry out to God in the middle of a dusty, fly-infested field.

My life of *comfort* is gone. I stress and I sweat and sometimes I wonder how the next bill will be paid. But I'm *content.* I'm content in Christ, because He strengthens me.

God called me to be a farmer. And guess what? He's calling you to something too. He's knocking on your door. He's whispering your name. You may think it sounds crazy at first. You may worry what people would say if you actually dared to listen. But you know what? Listen anyway. Follow.

The life you find may be strange and uncomfortable. It may be hard. It may push you to what you think is your breaking point and keep pushing you—pushing until you cry in pain and frustration and anger.

But follow anyway. It's only by following that you can find real contentment. It's only by following that you can find real purpose.

For all the work I do, for all the weariness that sinks and settles deep into my bones, I wake up every morning, look out the window, and feel . . . *amazed*. I can't believe that God allows me to steward this place. I can't believe how lucky I am. How blessed. I see the sun rise over my barn, the sky painted orange and purple. I hear the birds in the oak trees beyond. I breathe in the scent of the animals, the plants, the water in the air. And I feel God beside me. Above me. Everywhere.

The sun begins another day. The rooster crows. Every day brings its own trouble, yes, and my days can be filled with them. But they're filled with miracles too. Love. Peace. Family. Hope. Purpose.

On my twenty-seventh birthday, in a mansion in St. Louis, I stared into a mirror and saw my brother looking back at me.

Jason, what are you doing with your life that's so great? he said. *What are you doing with your life that's so awesome?*

I had no answers then.

I do now.

Acknowledgments

Special thanks to:

- Wester Farms
- The Rose brothers
- Society of St. Andrew
- Nash Produce
- Louisburg Tractor
- The many thousands of volunteers who have helped to grow, harvest, and donate more than one million pounds of food. For your humble hearts and service in love, I am forever grateful.

About the Author

Jason Brown grew up in Henderson, North Carolina. He went on to attend the University of North Carolina, where he played both guard and tackle before moving to center. He never missed a game. He was drafted in the fourth round by the Baltimore Ravens in 2005. Brown became a free agent in 2009 and was signed by the St. Louis Rams for $37.5 million, making him the highest-paid center in the league at the time. He was again a free agent three years later, but rather than signing a new contract, he left the NFL and bought a thousand-acre farm near Louisburg, North Carolina. Brown has been farming full time since 2013, and he gives nearly everything that he grows (mostly sweet potatoes) to the poor. He and his wife, Tay, have been married since 2003 and have eight children.

About the Type

This book was set in Sabon, a typeface designed by the well-known German typographer Jan Tschichold (1902–74). Sabon's design is based upon the original letter forms of sixteenth-century French type designer Claude Garamond and was created specifically to be used for three sources: foundry type for hand composition, Linotype, and Monotype. Tschichold named his typeface for the famous Frankfurt type-founder Jacques Sabon (c. 1520–80).

Dear Friend,

Tay and I founded Wisdom for Life and First Fruits Farm to share the love of Christ with our local communities and aid in hunger relief efforts in eastern North Carolina. Our goal is to have a light that shines brightly, and we encourage others to do the same by joining in our mission to "Never stop giving! Never stop loving! Never stop growing!" It's that simple.

To learn more about our family and unique mission, please visit the following websites:

wisdomforlife.org
faithfamilyfarming.com
amazinggrazeevents.com

Jason Brown

Philippians 4:13